HERITAGE

HERITAGE

CLAN OF
TUBAL CAIN
An Anthology

Thoth Publications

Frontispiece image Mermaid from 18th century Chapbook,
public domain

Published by Thoth Publications
2 Copt Oak Cottage, Whitwick Road, Markfield,
Leicestershire LE67 9QB

ISBN 9781913660390
Web address: www.thothpublications.com
Email: enquiries@thoth.co.uk

CONTENTS

1. Master of Reality   9
   ROBIN –THE-DART

2. Progressive Stasis   27
   ULRIC 'GESTUMBLINDI' GODING

3. Silence of the Gods   36
   LOUIS BOURBON

4. So What Are We Crafting?   40
   ULRIC 'GESTUMBLINDI' GODING

5. The Mead of Poetry   48
   SHANI OATES

6. The Nine Knots   82
   GRAEME SHACKLEFORD (KITH)

7. The Word Made Flesh   111
   MATTHEW JOHNSON (KITH)

8. Strength in Your Arms   120
   ULRIC 'GESTUMBLINDI' GODING

9. Sacred Dance & Sacred Fire   121
    SHANI OATES

10. Of Skalds, Scops & Puns   143
    SHANI OATES

11. Fool   150
    LOUIS BOURBON

12. In the Name of the Mask   154
    LOUIS BOURBON

13. Re-Forge & Temper   158
    ULRIC 'GESTUMBLINDI' GODING

14. Providence   162
    CHARLES F. SMITH

15. A Life Well Lived   169
    ULRIC 'GESTUMBLINDI' GODING

16. One   174
    ROBIN –THE-DART

17. Elegy For the Fallen   178
    ROBIN –THE-DART

Dedicated to all Seekers of
True Arte & Craft

*"To seek the divine one needs 'Faith, Courage and
Surrender'; Dignity not Fear, Confidence not Arrogance
Power not Force. Be careful what you pretend to Be, because
you are what you pretend to be. We do not accept any one
true Faith, the only requirement is that People find God
within themselves. What a Faith should not demand is
religious adherence and dogma, but truth and Purity of
Thinking. And always be of 'Pure Heart, Pure Mind
and Pure Speech."*

ROBIN-THE-DART

MASTER OF REALITY

"What any of us knows, is not necessarily what can be proved. But if it is true, then facts will be found to support that Truth. If these cannot be found, then what we know, is false. Knowledge is not wisdom, and one should never be mistaken for the other."

ROBIN-THE-DART

To be included within this small book that speaks of our heritage, where my own words rest alongside those of others whom I hold in great esteem, is a great privilege. My submission to the works of the 'People' is my thanks to them, for their grace and tenacity of spirit. As a Clan we have faced down so much adversity, and in enduring have found our cause ever deeper and stronger. It is an honour to hold the knots and mark the tides of man and of the gods in their unruly symbiosis.

I am duly grateful for a life 'lived' by the hearth-fire of my Craft ancestors, all of whom are deeply respected and held in memory and in thought too, for there is no purpose in one without the other if we are ever to move forward into the future. In this I take up the staff held by others before me and draw my thoughts and words into being that others may take or discard them, according to their Wyrð. Many things should be common knowledge; experience has proven they are not. The duty of the Head-kinsman is to care for the People to the utmost of his capabilities and then more. To coerce them to their best, to care for their needs, and to represent the Law – to maintain as great a balance around the Clan as possible. Holding together the concept of a People is incredibly important, for it is the mainstay of the People. Not to make comparisons that in any way suggest superiority, it is essential to stress how hugely different to the concept of Wicca, and lodge-based systems, a Traditional Clan People truly are. Too many systems profess to share their knowledge with initiates – but of what, exactly?

An eclectic mystery at best. Sage wisdom is best acquired within a hereditary lived tradition, in which many generations have evolved. This makes them relevant in the now, and understood through the needs of the now, which may be very different to those our revered ancestors wrapped their Wyrð around. Confusion arises when the imperative of time is ignored.

Greedily snatching at pearls from another's tradition will never inform your own. Any culture grows by absorption – over time. Subtle changes arrive naturally, sudden implementation causes alarm and confusion, the mind rejects always what it cannot immediately recognize or understand. Change occurs organically. Hence wisdom is a time-honoured treasure.

For almost two decades we have struggled against countless odds and onslaughts simply to observe the natural 'right' to be who we are. That is to say, not what others claim for us, nor in our name.

Fate and Tradition in Tandem [1]

What we do is our business and it is ours to tend and nurture, develop and change as we grow in time. What we do is 'our thing'. It is as simple as that. Ours. We defend our Faith. And despite having to raise the Guiden behind the shield wall, we have continued to do the work, all of this in the face of wild claims and desperate efforts to undermine the ancestral stream. Oddly enough, no one has had the wit to wonder why this might be.

We urge people to look to the source through clear connections, join the dots – the evidence is damning, charlatans one to a man, with much to lose. Meanwhile, we carry on regardless.

1. Woodcuts from 18th-Century Chapbooks. Public Domain.

But let us be clear, should anything they espouse ever materialize beyond their fain rhetoric, then yes, by all means shall we engage them in discourse. In other words, we politely request that those who seek to place themselves in opposition to our history or to challenge it in any way: please do us the courtesy to either put up or shut up. Apparently, requisite evidence is so very thin on the ground, the only word used against us thus far is 'secret' – an illusory possession of no possible use in any claim or comment except to the contrary.

All nonsense aside, our history, that is, the greater history of this Island's 'People,' is genuinely quite illuminating. Caesar in particular found Germania fascinating. In his studies, he noted that separate tribes of people ranked in similarity of their Gods. So what was Caesar's understanding that seems to have escaped the attention of so many of the great Crafters' of today? He recognized their individuality. They were not an homogeneity. Coming from a Clan based tradition himself (Clan Julii) he knew an ancestral Faith when he saw one.

All of them literally 'followed the gods of their father's fathers.' Of course, this is perhaps a very disconcerting concept for many modern Pagans who might otherwise assume an over-arching or worse, eclectic pantheon for their presumed 'Golden-Age.' The brutality and individuality prevalent in the past, overtly enhanced in the 'now,' should hopefully cause them to sharply draw breath and consider what exactly do they believe they are recreating or returning to and reviving?

Each Tribe and Clan had their own ancestors that intervened on their behalf, personal to them alone. Very much family traditions, no two families shared quite the

The Rus [2]

same view of their gods, or told quite the same tales or myths about them. Rather like the many Clans that 'People' the Indian Sub-continent, erroneously referred to as 'Hindu's. Neither the 'people' nor the 'faith' they subscribe to is 'Hindu.' Refuting that homogeneity, they do not refer to themselves by that term. Why-ever would they?

Their differences do not imply a schism, because there never was an 'orthodoxy.' Each Clan has a particular family name that ties them to variations of a Faith whose deified entities express myriad faces and guises, names and legends. The problem resides with the modern mind-set that has the over-worked tendency to look backwards through

2. Woodcut. Public Domain

13

the lens of Christianity and other single based Faiths and thusly presume for them, an orthopraxy.

This standard form is made the yard-stick by which non-conformists are factions and schisms, and where everyone subscribes to one set of names for their gods denoting distinct pantheons. It was never thus in the ancient world. Our communities, if we can still call them that, are so regulated and entirely drained of individualism, we have indeed long-forgotten who 'the gods of our father's fathers' were, and who we, as individual Peoples were.

For them, you were part of one family or another, and lived accordingly. NO schisms, NO factions, No separation

Symbel [3]

3. Image stone from Gotland, in the Swedish Museum of National Antiquities in Stockholm. Public Domain. Wiki-commons license.

of a People; you belonged or you did not, and you belonged through birth or adoption. Either way you were bound to those People by a Troth of allegiance. Or you did not, and you belonged elsewhere, be that cast out as an outlaw, or wolfs-head; or you belonged to another tribe altogether and were named for them.

Names were important, because they delineated 'boundaries, of land, of People, of Faith and of their Gods.

So you see, historically, it is impossible to claim to be 'of a People' unless you truly are, and that means you live amongst them. Succinct and economical, it requires no further explanation. The best thing is that no-one's tradition or customs, or gods or name even, could be stolen. No-one would actually want to, and outside any particular family, these things would mean nothing at all.

Of course, this does not mean any could or should claim to have or hold a lineage back to Boudicca, or even that we should be taken seriously.

What it does mean, is that an honourable way of working instigated tomorrow is more valid than any two thousand years old if corrupted. Only Truth matters; seeking to live in the rightness of things. And so I ask, is this a terrible thing to stand for, to live for our own natural culture, Northern at the heart and core, overlaid with other subtleties that have shaped us into who we are, who are fathers were? We hold to no prejudice; our Faith is without hatred and without malice, but we are willing to stand by the sword and the shield to defend it. The People are now so few; this belief and way of 'life' is sadly now almost extinct. A grim reality.

We hold to our own, our ancestors, and to their beliefs. We follow our ancestors through the skies, we observe their passing, watch their camp fires, and bless them when they are gathered up home again. Whenever we hold ritual,

Saga and Óðinn [4]

we need to see the sky, whatever the location. Thus when Evan John Jones once said that any one, in truth could simply stand alone, beneath the stars and Moon, raise a cup to those chosen to receive their dedication, it is just

4. Robert Engels – 1919. Public Domain Wiki Commons License

as valid as any raised in Companie – he meant just that! Not everyone can have access to open space, but this does not negate individual responsibility to acknowledge one's roots, always. For our own tradition, we make no excuses for its idiosyncrasies.

The Mistress or Clan Mother is normally chosen because of her gift of the sight. She is the Maid, the Seeress and Prophetess, the Sybil.

Therefore, she holds the Egregore, the spiritual space, to maintain balance and harmony in the rightness of things. She mediates the Egregore and the Old Ones as the representative of the divine spirit for the People. The Tannist, Lawful Son, holds the Priestly Rites and relevant Law for the People. His Charge is to be their spiritual guide, and share the Clan's lore and customs, its Mythos, the dreams and aspirations of our cumulative ancestors, and its evolution through a millennia of change.

His duties are manifold. He is the needful diplomat, spokesperson and envoy for the Clan. By contrast, the Head-Kinsman meters THE Law, administering justice when needful. He has full authority over all others as Leader of the Clan. He is responsible for the welfare and well-being of his People.

He is the Father and representative this side of the river, of all the Clan's ancestors. Beyond those duties, beyond his Clan, he has no interest in popularity or even notoriety. He holds and embodies the virtue of the 'Word' as the Law for his People. Beyond that, his Tannist is the contact point between The People and the outside world.

The Head-Kinsman stands against those who would attack the People, and not always in a visible form. Seeing nothing of what he does, does not mean nothing is being done; there should never be a desire to broadcast private matters, nor to seek the attention of a public audience.

'The Gossip – Wagging Tongues'[5]

Circumstances will eventually dictate the 'need' of such enterprise – or not. All those we have been forced to consider as transgressors are held in equal levels of compassion and severity, and the response is meted as deemed necessary and appropriate. My duty is clear. Like

5. *Emperor's New Clothes'* by Thomas Heath Robinson, 1899, (in *Fairy tales from Hans Christian Andersen*) Public Domain, wiki commons license.

John (E.J.J) and Doreen (Valiente), I believe we have to stand up for the good of the Craft, which means watching each other's backs; always. Sociopaths, charlatans and other manner of fakes and wannabe's will always slither their way into places that give them the opportunity to exploit others.

All of us need to be vigilant to maintain the credibility of the Craft. Everyone suffers the possibility of exposure by a hostile media; so we must not let them hang us all to dry for a minority of undesirable miscreants. They have to be routed, exposed then exiled, and unless we are willing to do this together, as a collective, then one by one, we will all fall. It is a given.

Freedom for all is a wonderful thing, but these people can and will take liberties, literally. If any of us believe we have a heritage of any value or merit, then we must muster a policy of Zero tolerance - we should never settle for less. I know I won't.

Remembering how so many of today's occultists are merely keyboard warriors and craft experts, declaring far and wide their wondrous prowess, we should again apply common sense, and choose to observe certain reality checks. Delusion is contagious, especially when marketed with esteem and prestige – 'Emperor's new Clothes' and all that.

Truth 'really' is infinitely more rewarding – in absolute terms, both tangible and experiential. No amount of 'likes' and sycophancy can ever equal that. A sense of pride in extending care to others should never be considered unnecessary, nor a bad thing. This is what builds true community, something we have lost and may never regain. The Faith is our birth-right, belittled and side-lined by more profitable enterprises. If we fall at any level, we fall

Smith Craft [6]

6. *The Forging of Balmung* by Howard Pyle, Public domain, Wiki Commons License.

all the way. Once divided, we become an ever decreasing society, community, family etc. until we are insular individuals – impotent and without voice. There was a time when mankind believed in the reality of a Utopia, which devolved into the utopian dream, and now remains only in distant memory of even that. Myths and legends were generated in the virtue of that hope.

These principles forged a truly golden age — the belief and faith in that 'New Age' – the era of all possible realities where humanity existed within and alongside its gods. Without this belief, dream or hope, we may as well all be dead, for we shall never rise amongst the quick!

Therefore, we do hold fast to those primal and arcane beliefs, hopes and dreams, and aspire to make them our universal reality. Our ancestors did no less, and we expect no less of our descendants.

We hold the line for Truth, Love and Beauty. We stand as a beacon; we maintain the 'Need-Fire,' and we honour and treasure the gifts and skills and the sacred lore of our humanity in dutiful Heritage. Oddly these principles are what we have been desperately trying to hold onto for decades, and have found ourselves under constant attack for. Why would that be, when we seek no others' tradition, we have our own. We do not claim anyone's work or material; we have our own.

And yet to honour and live our own Tradition seems to make (some) others' envious. For example, a few years ago, on the anniversary of E.J.J.'s death we wished to set up a small

Watcher at the Ford [7]

Craft exhibition in commemoration of his contribution to the Clan's heritage at the 'Museum of Witchcraft.' We were quite startled to receive an unenthusiastic response from its then curator Mr. Graham King, whose reply was a curt:

"Do you think the museum is the right place for your type of thing."

Too flabbergasted to respond with dignity, I never did find out what exactly is the right type of thing according to him, so left the matter without comment. But it does illustrate the form barriers can take when something else is in play.

Honour, is definitely thin on the ground, it would seem. There is no bitterness in relaying these things, simply to inform what is widely unknown.

7. *Bunworth Banshee, Fairy Legends and Traditions of the South of Ireland'* by Thomas Crofton Croker, 1825. Public Domain, Wiki Commons License.

Almost all those protagonists have now cast their pennies to the ferryman, serving Wyrð in other ways as they stand before their own gods to face a greater Reality and Truth, which thankfully, is their concern. They are no longer mine. And so with the base line marked we can move on to the future.

I make no apologies for our Tradition, it is unique. Perhaps we are a dying breed. Time will tell. To those who seek its path, and adopt its known and public works, I task only with the honesty in acknowledging their source out of courtesy.

Technology has joined the dots and so the World may seem a smaller place. But this matters not in the ways of Tradition, where, like Roy and John before me, all is passed by word of mouth. We have remained true to the old customs, and though I am not active in the world of media hyperbole, I certainly am in the Ring of Arte. My duty is to the shadows. The light is held by my Tannist son, and he is my bridge to the outer world; for he is my eyes and ears there.

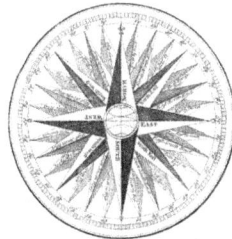

Star Compass[8]

Our tradition is written in the stars, it can be seen within the Eddas, within the folklore of centuries past and in the mythos as it yet evolves – it is far greater than the sum of its parts. Our Mythos, our ancestors, our Round of Life, is mapped out in the Realms of the Gods, and that includes the land beneath our feet. All things serve as a mnemonic to

8. Compass rose detail from 1748 *Bowen Mariner's Compass and Armillary Sphere – Geographicus* – Circle of Winds-bowen-1747. Public Domain, Wiki Commons License.

them and their rites in ways that reveal a complex theology and mythology. They are SEEN and easily remembered, by ourselves, and by those before us, some of whom were not necessarily educated – and I mean educated as opposed to being intelligent which is something else entirely; the two are not necessarily inclusive or compatible. To understand the Compass is to understand our cultural history its growth and evolution, its layers, not as an intellectualism, though at its core it holds a very specific sentience – a Craft intelligence. This understanding can take many years and that is no blind, truly, years.

Only when fully understood is the pilgrim able to move onto the next stage. It is pointless engaging the Compass unless this is understood. Anyone can hold festival and celebration, dedication to the Gods even, but if there is no understanding of what is being done, then all that *is* done, is a pointless engagement with 'space' – where one is simply going round in circles. What we seek to engage are our dearest kin, those we remain linked to in spirit once they have passed beyond the Ring. They are our direct link through a physical then spiritual bond. In turn they become the 'Shadow Companie' (because they are never hidden from us) linked through the Egregore, who link to the Old Ones, who ford the bridge to the Egregore, that's held by the Maid – and into the house that Jack built we go.

Understanding each vital role adopted by our officers and banner-men alongside personal symbols that reveal and convey our Mythos, essentially develops an 'other' mask, integral to it.

Each brother or sister is taught the virtue our totems, each rune and sign upon the door, the purpose of totemic Masks, who the Disir are, where to seek the gate and hold the Knot; what words to speak to the Guardian at the Gate; how to scribe their symbol upon THE Mask; at what point of the Compass each Stellar trajectory is engaged; where to seek the Dragon's Pearl; and how to scry the Eye of Wyrð. Without such treasure, then the Ferry, the Ferry-man and the distant destination will forever elude us – as we are not worth a light.

In vibrant expression of our 'lived' tradition, Roy Bowers composed an edifying poem, unseen by ourselves until more recent events led to its 'happen-chance' discovery. Exposed to ourselves through the unwitting machinations of others, Roy states a crucial part of our Mythos, overlooked completely by those who'd previously held it. What he

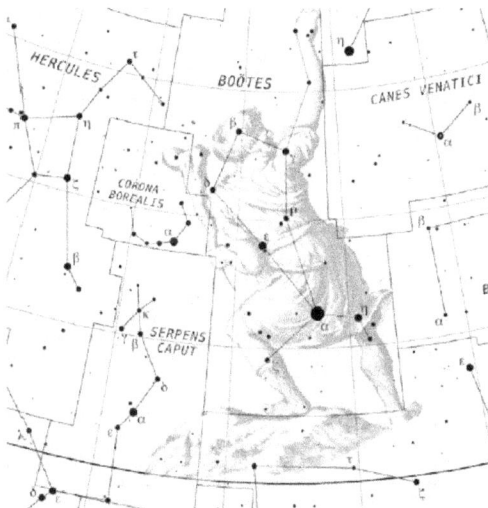

Ophiuchus seu Serpentarius, Coelum Stellatum[9]

9. 1801, Public Domain, Wiki Commons License.

illustrates is perfectly clear to our eyes at least – but only because we 'live' the tradition. He speaks of the keys to his Tradition to someone who sadly had absolutely no idea what he was talking about. Yet fifty years later it could have been written today, for those who People his Clan still. It speaks of symbolism, of Fate, the Gods, the Compass, how to access it, engage it and of its hidden Mysteries – all the things our ancestors observed in Wyrð.

That enigmatic poem may be read within *Tubal's Mill*, the Clan's auto-biography.

With erstwhile humour I leave you with this, John's best quote:

"Bullshit baffles brains, never bullshit a bull-shitter, and NEVER bullshit someone who knows more than you do."

Enough said.

PROGRESSIVE STASIS

"I write this not as merely a follower of a praxis distinct in its technology but as a member of a People distinct in its culture. The horns are set, the fork in hand. Time to be a rascal and play Devil's Advocate..."

All men are **not** equal.

Sickly sweet utopian gushing.

Keep bleating in the growing flock, sheep will remain sheep and wolves will still act accordingly. As much as one wills it otherwise, this cannot change. Sheep may be appeased and invited into the lair, but they will be picked off for supper when the need or want arises.

The fixation of self, any subsequent navel-gazing seems to have disarmed the 'western world'. We look to uphold a political correctness, all the while we live under a politic that fails many. We watch threats strengthen as we squabble to determine what right-action is.

Due to the 'progressive' nature of Western society, there

are as many different opinions as there are individuals; so much so that progression toward resolution falters and becomes static. Strength in common identity will always have the upper hand.

Yet how many in this 'forward-faring' world can say that they 'add' to a community?

It is not a collection of individuals that make a community, but a collection of smaller cohesive units, families if you like.

Though being a human—being is a shared trait amongst us, we are not a homogeneous blob. The make-up of, not only humanity, but also the multitude of life's expression in this world is heterogeneous and should be welcomed as such.

Are we looking at conversion attempts, preachings from yet more

Twelfth Night[10]

10. *The King Drinks* –1650 and 1660 By David Tenniers. Public Domain, Wiki Commons License.

'prophets', radical-this, liberal-that, manifestos a-plenty looking to marry Craft with secular humanism? If you do not accept 'this', then you are not 'truly' following that… Whose authority dictates that such is the case?

Has 'Traditional' or Old Craft had its day?

Traditional worldviews are exclusive in their nature, such is the nature of the beast; ask any anthropologist and I'm sure they will tell you the same. One is either within accepted societal or (sub-) cultural bounds or they are not, and if outside of them then one is literally an 'Outsider' by default.

Personally, I may wander the landscape, share the company of others, benefit from outside hospitality, yet I remain distinct from them. I am bound to my People's Law, I find my kinship in the People, I owe my fealty to the Maid and Magister of the Clan. Others' have their own bonds and boundaries in which I do not share and so I am an "Outsider" to them and their kind, as they are outside to mine.

I understand that these are not comfortable words in a world which demands inclusiveness; yet this is the reality to those who adhere to a Traditional paradigm.

The Sisters decided my lot in this lifetime at my first breath, in probability long before then. If I wasn't born a particular colour, creed or so on and that bars me from entrance into an indigenous system or culture then so be it, Wyrð has spoken. The problem doesn't lie with exclusivity but the violence or lack of tolerance shown in either the maintenance of exclusivity, or the enforcement of inclusiveness. For example, is it 'wrong' if First Nation People wish to keep their practices exclusive to their own kin?

In my opinion, it is not; yet can that exclusive behaviour be argued as racist? I will leave that for each to mull over for themselves.

It seems to be a modern phenomenon that people think that the world owes them something, that by merely being born human we "have a right" to everybody's culture or sub-cultures. Well here is news to those folk; the World owes you nothing. Through your actions alone may you acquire your allotted portion in life and not by simply existing as a member of humanity.

The harsh reality of life is that we are not born equal, intellectually or physically we do not develop homogeneously, each have their own strengths and weakness that may benefit and hinder as one traverses the path from birth to death. To those who seek solace in the Cult of the Individual this is an uncomfortable prospect; this would mean that one is 'better' suited than another in different stations within societal make-up. To those who adhere to a Traditional worldview, this isn't an uncomfortable outlook to be replaced by a liberal inclusiveness; this is simply common reality where disparate parts forge a stronger whole.

For too long have people been paddling in a New-Age sewage that is 'self-seeking', 'self-development', self,

Prometheus[11]

11. Gustave Moreau, 1869. Public domain, via Wikimedia Commons License

self, self… Benefiting one's self as a priority, the material evolution of roots founded in the selfish eschatology that is 'personal salvation'.

I look around the Craft 'community' and I see multitudes of individuals seeking to 'make a name for themselves' for their own sake, to be a mover and shaker within the sphere of the Craft. Self-professed Magisters, Councils, and Manifestos declared which aggrandise the authors more than getting arses off couches and away from the screens. I hear with a disheartening consistency;

"my relationship with the spirits gives me…", or "I will do a working to get…",or "I will buy this limited edition snake skin book…".

What a charade; it seems that we comfortable folk of the 21st century are playing Harry Potter so that we can out-boast another faceless avatar on the Internet. That which people are play-acting Craft to be, is little more than flapping arms about, listening to empty echoes of one's own chatter and inflating egos as we brag to all who will listen.

This is a far cry from what endears me to the Craft. Lost in petty distraction, this quest to build a persona accepted by peers has done more to damage than build anything lasting. The Cult of Personality is a sickly-sweet poison indeed, just like the sweeteners in artificial foods, you can't feel it killing you.

One's precious view of self means very little, at best a charismatic persona will allow the spread of ideas which may benefit community – at worse a charismatic personality can cause atrocities such as those suffered during the WW2 era, as well as eras prior and eras to come.

Persona is merely a tool, it enables interaction, it hopefully gives one the means to benefit one's community.

The Conjurer [12]

A workman isn't defined by their tools, nor should we be fascinated by the tool that is ego.

Robert Cochrane, an ancestor of my People and founder of the Clan, has been subject to this personality cult since his passing, many want a piece of him so to speak.

Please allow me to be somewhat controversial for a moment…

Who he was, outside of his own People, is of no

12. *Historia Mundi Naturalis*, Plinii Secundi. 1582 Public Domain, Wiki Commons License.

consequence; yes, he was gifted, he was tormented also. I'm sure that there are plenty who share these traits in the world. What matters more are his *ideas*, things that have survived and strengthened since his death, ideas that have *given inspiration* to many, ideas that have *strengthened a larger community* rather than just benefit the lonely island of one's self. The Craft is about relationship, plain and simple. Yes, the Egoic-self gives us an initial orientation point as we take our compass and journey across the vast landscapes of human and other-than-human existence. But it serves as an initial orientation only. Relationships are not solely concerned with taking, but a reciprocal giving.

The Craft is a natural expression of culture, traditionally one rooted in gift-giving, which strengthened bonds within community (between both human and Other), this in turn gave better odds of survival against outside threat, whether in the form of famine or violence.

Let me reiterate, however, not so much the survival of self, but the survival of a people.

If we are not vigilant, the Cult of Individuality will bring the death of Traditional Craft. It matters not a jot whether one is gay, straight, trans-, black, white, yellow; pro-this or anti-that, is but further entrenchment within self.

Embrace heterogeneity but never lose sight that rather than serving self, *seek to serve your people*, your community, first and foremost. And for those who would profess themselves Magister, Summoner, Man in Black, or other titles, remember that such titles should remind you that you hold further responsibility in service to your people, hold them as:

'A yoke of necessity rather than a boon of status.'

Whatever titles, distinctions or orientations of self are held, they soon disappear when a blade is held at the neck.

It is not an impending loss of straightness, gayness, whiteness or blackness that we fear in this fatal circumstance, it is the loss of Life which we mourn.

After all…

"*Nobody has much use for a corpse.*" [13]

Dans Macabre [14]

13. (Hávamál) 14. *The Pedlar*, from '*Dance of Death. 1538*, in – *A Brief History of Wood-engraving from its Invention* Joseph Cundall, 1895. Public Domain, Wiki Commons License

SILENCE OF THE GODS

We are human beings equipped with the same vital organs and brain as very other human being. Our connection is an innate need and desire for Truth which leads to Knowledge and Wisdom.

This is the Brick we individually craft and bear. It leads us to each other and to a common desire to lay our bricks to build a common Hearth for Ourselves.

The first brick to this particular Hearth was laid by Roy Bowers.

Midway upon the journey of our life I found myself within a forest dark, for the straightforward pathway had been lost.

This poetically describes the approach towards an individual's passage into 'Initiation,' into the way of the gods. All Initiations are said to require an avatar; the mediatrix, the facilitator - sometimes also described in terms of an 'otherworldly' manifestation in spirit to sign the post and illuminate our path.

Just like Dante, this writer found himself somehow lost at a certain stage in his life. And just like Dante, a saviour came forward in the form of a lucid dream.

Little knowing at that time who the oneiric person was, I would eventually discover our spiritual existences had in fact been entwined forever. Though unknown, these things were known.......and felt. Though unspoken, they were heard. As ever, the first experience of force unbeknownst to me then, had manifested itself already via the sacred analogue of all Mysteries:

1. Poetic Vision. As explained by Robert Cochrane, this is intuitive perception via dreams or trance work with no use of logic or reason.

This was the beginning of a journey. What followed, was a recognition of 'people', symbols, places, words etc, all from an 'otherwise' past I had not knowingly experienced before.

At this time I had met the Maid of the Clan and it is now, in retrospect, beyond logic how quickly the second experience of force had come about.

This is known to us as:

2. Vision of Memory.

3. Magical Vision. Work in earnest had begun. Hard work. Immersion in unfamiliar principles. Working in ways that brought more questions than answers. Fear sometimes for what was experienced was true to the core and in a world of illusion I felt out of my depth.

It is at this time that we truly understand that existence isn't what we thought before and there's no turning back as one cannot un-know or experience what one has known and experienced. Bewildering as it may feel, this is the time to go further than one thought possible.

After this, we discover:

Anima Mundi[15]

15. *Anima Mundi* by Robert Fludd, Public domain, via Wikimedia Commons license.

SILENCE OF THE GODS

4. Religious Vision. This is the true initiation. The right that eventually is performed and the Oaths that are taken are but the culmination of it, not the onset of the choice made.

It is the time when we first make contact with the Godhead. After this we become aware of the different levels of existence and embark on an eternal battle to conquer Fate.

5. Mystical Vision. This is the reward. The Grail if you like. Glimpsed only and elusive always. It is the full union with the Godhead. The total annihilation of ego. The illumination of Lucifer that expands beyond all possibility the form of being. This is in short part of our journey.

A journey travelled through experience, devotion, hard work. It is a solitary journey that we travel side by side. It cannot be taught orally as the world of the Gods is silent.

So, What Are We Crafting?

'Witchcraft Today' 50 years on...

"It is no measure of health to be well-adjusted to a sick society."

J. Krishnamurti

Fighting against ravaging elements, the underlying threat of invasion and brimming societal upheavel (due to the mechanisms of an economic elite), the peasant classes were subjected to tax upon tax, upon tax. Those words may sound as though they had been lifted from a description of feudal Europe; nevertheless, they fit rather aptly to Northern Europe, or 'the West' and beyond, in this the second decade of the 21st century.

"Witches cannot retreat from the world any longer, there is no room for us in this society, unless we have something valid to offer it, and participate in its social evolution."[16]

As one who lives Traditional Craft now in the 21st century, I find myself living, very much so, in a world exposed, metaphorical 'warts an' all'.

---

16. Robert Cochrane - 'Witchcraft Today'

The good, the bad and the ugly have no rock to hide beneath.

If one knows where to look or who to ask, anything may be brought to light and yet the vast majority are happy to abide in a willful ignorance. Ignorance is bliss – supposedly. This ignorance extends itself into the spheres of ecology, economy, politics (the Greek origin meaning "for, of, or relating to citizens) and ultimately an ignorance of Self.

It seems that this age is deeply entrenched in the glamour of persona, the media seems employed to celebrate the shallow and the lurid, quite literally the age of the "Celebrity". In an era of the celebrated individual and supposed instantaneous socio-global connection, a brooding dis-connection is most surely felt. With each person vying to stand alone atop of their respective summits we find that such insular dispersion has left an absence of community in its wake.

"The value of the Old Craft today is that in it lie the seeds of the old Mystery tradition. Through this, the witch may perceive the beginnings of that ultimate in wisdom, knowledge of themselves and of their motives."[17]

It seems paradoxical to the modern mind that the endeavour of knowing and working upon one's Self can benefit community as a whole; when undertaken with a noble and pure intent, Self-realization is indeed a thoroughly unselfish enterprise. Cochrane states in the quote above, that self-knowledge and knowledge of what

17. Robert Cochrane – *'Witchcraft Today'*

Sophianic Realms[18]

18. Sophia, Mystical, 'Secret figures of the Rosicrucians.' 1775. Public Domain, Wiki Commons License.

motivates one in their speech, thoughts and actions is the 'ultimate in wisdom.'

When speaking to other seekers on the path in regards to wisdom, I have stated that; Wisdom, I believe, must have the ability to be applied in this journey called "Life" in order to differentiate it from an abstract Knowledge. 'Gnosis' may lead to Wisdom for example; though there will be both cultural and perennial wisdoms, what may be wise practice for the desert may lead one to perish in the tundra for example.

Looking back to Cochrane's quote in this regard, highlights that self-knowledge in its fullest capacity enables one to live and die in the rightness-of-things, such knowledge cannot help but foster application in life and all of the interactions throughout. However, when the gold of gnosis births the virgin milk of Wisdom, it must be carried forward so as to not turn sour through stagnant pooling.

Incessant navel-gazing, or the pretty distraction of academic pursuit and the overt flexing of intellectual muscle is to risk the fate of Narcissus, drowning in the produce of our own eflection; hold in mind the wise-counsel of the Hávamál:

"... No-one has use for a corpse."[19]

I have been known to suggest that traversing the landscape of life may be viewed akin to wandering a labyrinth; we take a few steps forward, we step away, only then to find, in actuality, that we are now walking closer

19. (Hávamál St. 71)

Diana the Huntress [20]

20. *Diana the Huntress* – School of Fontainebleau, attributed to Luca Penni 1550.
Public Domain, Wiki Commons License.

toward the centre. Repeating the process, drawing ever closer. Closer to what?

You may ask...

Closer to that legendary crossroad where the 'Ol' Devil' finally gifts the worthy and the black sun shines dazzling at midnight! Closer to our Self; that inherent divinity!

"The Mysteries are, in essence, means by which man may perceive his own inherent divinity."[21]

What is key, thereafter, is that we do not then retreat into that omphalos of Self, the VITRIOL of Alchemists: '*Visita Interiora Rectificando Invenies Occultum Lapidem*' as the discovery therein is of immense worth to the World, and so it is imperative that we must then find our way back! The Hunter and Hunted are indeed One; the tested and realised Hero then follows Her thread back to the inhabited World.

Those who have embarked on such a quest, whether deemed successful or not, never return unchanged.

Upon surfacing from the labyrinthine cave, the battle-worn seeker may spend a length of time catching their breath whilst replaying the events that have now shaped them. Do they return to the World from which they had left in order to undertake this endeavor? Or do they form a hermitage built around the riches earned?

Are we to disassociate from the World or are we to live according to a realised Ideal, reforming first ourselves, then our people, and then, through an osmosis, the larger

---

21. Robert Cochrane – 'Witchcraft Today' See: *The Robert Cochrane Letters: The Star-Crossed Serpent III*, Shani Oates (Ed) 2016 Mandrake of Oxford.

community? What worth has gold if it is sat upon? It may have a comforting beauty to gaze upon but it only has that intrinsic worth to those who are fortunate enough to hold it. Hoarded-gold is frequently cursed gold in the old tales. Gift-giving, is a traditional custom that ensures the strength of bonds and health of a community. The gold of Gnosis when shared with upright intentions becomes the gift of Wisdom.

"If you bring forth what is within you, what you bring forth will save you. If you do not bring forth what is within you, what you do not bring forth will destroy you."[22]

Will the discerning Seeker recognise Her when they see Her?

If the Work hasn't been truly pursued then their "*doors of Perception*" shall not be cleansed and they will recoil and mock a supposed Hag in their midst. How woe shall befall such an individual! The Mother shall eat Her children, an uttered curse shall haunt their existence.

Yet, for them who are pure of intent, those whose perception is cleansed once more, the Parzivals of the world, will recognise that immaculate beauty of Eternal Wisdom and the Seeker shall bear the Wedding Garment. The kingdom shall rejoice, peace will be known, the Heiros Gamos realised. The dowry of which, is paid forward to the community that surrounds each of those who have been as One in the Wedding Chamber within.

---

22. Gospel of Thomas – 70

Alchemycal Weddyng [24]

"It may be that he will be desirous to follow us, and to enter into the Inner Choir, where the Soul joineth Hands and danceth with Sophia, or the Divine Wisdom." [23]

23. Jacob Boehme   24. *Sol moon*. Jaroš Griemiller, 1578. Public Domain, Wiki Commons License.

THE MEAD OF POETRY

"Myths are rarely to be taken literally; we must peel away the husk to reveal the kernel of wisdom within. The word is veiled and must be charmed from its refuge, paradise after all is a place of hidden wonders, bathed in eternal and effulgent light, such a garden once graced the pages of many sacred books. The mystic fire of heaven – divine grace, life, fertility, a gardener to oversee it all. The Tree of Life and Knowledge. This garden earth. The truth is really very simple. The ploughman rises in the skies above, a heavenly pedagogue, there for all with eyes to see. His tale is woven over the ensuing seasons as he moves across the skies and descends briefly before rising again. A perpetual reminder of the cycle of things; of life within eternity. But the seasons are merely a temporal cycle of life upon which is reflected the greater eternal cycle of the cosmos, of the stars and the heavens of both our ancestors and our descendants. Thus, the ritual year unfolds, a panoply of reflected gnosis." [25]

---

25. Robin-the-Dart

Norse folk-tales are renowned for their remarkable ability to totally absorb us within the very fantastical juxtaposition between what appears to be the far reaches of possibility and the quite un-extraordinary commonalities wherein the gods live and walk among us.

Very succinctly they illustrate the wily cunning employed by all means fair or foul to preserve divine potential for humanity to know and remember the reason for its being. The following tale is no exception. It beautifully explores the sublime subtlety of the many veiled layers, revealing just enough that we might be better prepared for all that fate places before us. As seekers of a shared and ultimate destiny, we discover it withheld closest to the seed.

Scattered clues, integral to the plot, lend support to a conceivable origin for our most enduring agricultural traditions. Celebrated within the 'Nine Men's Morris' leaping dance/ game once performed on the threshing floor, further mysteries abound.

In like manner, it shares a conjoined enigma with the rite of *'Crying the Neck'* for which no extant meaning has been awarded nor satisfactorily explained. When seen upon the hand as the symbol for the *'The Round of Life'* generated by traditions still marked and held in close accord within our Clan, we may shift towards an exploration of their incumbent mysteries through: *life, love, maturity, death and resurrection.*

It is quite be-fitting then, to note how the index finger, attributed to Jove, representing Hoary Wisdom and justice, is the fulcrum and pinnacle of this natural penta-grammatic graphic.

"POETIC VISION, in which the participant has inward access to dream images and symbols.

This is the result of the unconscious being stimulated by various means. Images are taught as part of a tradition, and also exist (as Jung speculated) upon their own levels. They are, when interpreted properly, means by which a lesser part of truth may be understood." [26]

HOW ÓÐINN WON THE MEAD

Eventually, the long wars between the Æsir and the Vanir ceased and all the gods sealed their truce by spitting into a great jar from which they fashioned a man, gifted in the art and wit of the gods; he was named Kvasir. Steeped deeply in the knowledge of the nine worlds, his wisdom was of such great renown he attracted many in need of his instruction. His travels took him through all worlds and realms, wandering far and wide until one day he found himself the guest of two dwarves, by whose hands he was fated to meet his death. They killed him, then after draining his blood into two large jars and a cauldron, they added honey to brew the finest and most divine mead.

All who would drink of it became wise in the poetic arts. But the dwarves decided to keep the mead (and its wisdoms) for themselves and when a messenger from the gods was sent forth to ask after Kvasir's well-being and whereabouts, the tale given was that he had died, choking, as a consequence of his wisdom. Later still, it happened that two giants were also slaughtered by the dwarves, but their son, Suttung searched relentlessly for them.

26. Roy Bowers

Finding the trail ended with the dwarves Suttung pronounced their execution, but they begged for mercy. This was granted in lieu of three containers of the divine soma/mead. These were very quickly taken to his Mountain home where they were hidden and guarded by his daughter Gunnloð by day and by night.

Óðinn, upon hearing of the whereabouts of this remarkable treasure, decided to recover it himself and journeyed to Jötunheim disguised as a man by the name of Bölverkr (grief worker).

Virtue of the Blood [27]

27. *The Dead Kvasir,* by Frank Stassen, 1920. Public Domain, Wiki Commons License.

Eventually he arrived at a valley where he encountered nine men in a field scything the harvest. Bölverkr being very aware the slow progress of their toil was due only to their blunted scythes, offered to show them how to sharpen them in order to become more efficient.

Using his whetstone, he also demonstrated how to care for the blades upon which their livelihood depended. Bölverkr soon learned that these men were working for Suttung's brother Baugi.

Reapers a gatherin' in [28]

Recognising at once an opportunity when all the reapers wished to buy the whetstone from Bölverkr, he responded by throwing it high into the air above them, declaring it a fitting trophy for the winner. Jumping up, they all span around; as they jostled for the prize, turning, one by one, they simultaneously cut each other's throats falling down dead in a heap amongst the wheaten grass.

28. 'KHira_Pyø' from "Book of Ruth" of Francysk Skaryna between 1517 and 1519. Public Domain, Wiki Commons License.

Bölverkr caught up his whetstone and continued his journey in search of the sacred mead.[29]Reaching Baugi's farm, he requested hospitality from the giant, who was not in good humour, for having lost his team of nine reapers, he knew he had no one else to complete the harvest. Bölverkr/Óðinn offered his help in return for some of the mead his brother Suttung stored in the mountain.

This made Baugi uneasy as he was sure his brother would refuse this request. Even though Bölverkr completed the harvest in double-quick time, Suttung refused, just as Baugi had suspected. Bölverkr eventually persuaded Baugi to assist him in his mission to steal some of the treasured mead. They drilled into the mountain, creating a tunnel just large enough for Óðinn to slither into, in the form of a snake. Whilst in this form, Baugi attempted unsuccessfully to skewer him with the drill. Once inside, he restored his form to that of a man and began immediately to charm Gunnlöð, still faithfully guarding the mead for her father.

And so for three days, they spent much time in one anothers' company within the mountain, by which time, she was eager to give him anything he desired. Asking for three drinks of the precious mead, he swallowed, first the huge jar, then the next jar and finally the cauldron. With the treasure held fast within his mouth, Óðinn changed himself into an eagle, flying off towards Ásgarðr. But

---

29.The whetstone signifies the obligation of reciprocity held by a liege lord, displaying his authority over the guilds and fecundity round all four cardinal points. This is well demonstrated in the Sutton Hoo burial grave-goods that included the highly prized whetstone of the King; it is crowned by a stag, the divine psychopomp and sacred symbol of kingship, beneath which four faces surround the staff.

Óðinn steals the Mead [30]

Suttung witnessed the transformation and also became an eagle, giving angry chase. As they approached Ásgarðr, the other gods, seeing both eagles, placed three large containers out for Óðinn to spit out the mead into.

This is stored still by the gods as just reward for those in Óðinn's gift (of divine poetry and wisdom). A few

30. Illustration by Jakob Sigurðsson 18th C. Public Domain, Wiki Commons License.

precious drops leaked out and are even now considered as the 'rhymester's share '(or portion of an inferior poet).[31]

WHERE THIS FITS TODAY

"THE VISION OF MEMORY, in which the devotee not only remembers past existence but also, at times, a past perfection." [32]

This ponderous tale reflects very well the importance of the wisdom mead within the histories and mythologies of Northern Traditions, illustrating how wisdom may be won, via cunning and wit.

Óðinn is herein attributed with using disguise and deception to obtain his prize – though neither are noble traits.

They en-flesh his ambivalent character, one that makes

Seers and Storytellers

31. See Scoffing & Punning. 32. Roy Bowers Image: *Home Again! The story of a life in Rebel prison – Harper's Weekly* 1865. [wood engraving – artists unknown] Public Domain, Wiki Commons License.

sense only in the whole context of his obligation to retrieve the mead of poetry (wisdom) by any means fair or foul that secures it as a free and accessible right of all men. Since the gods first furnished mankind with free thought and with this gift of wisdom, then no being, of god or man is lawful in keeping such a treasure hoarded for themselves alone. Fragments of this tale survive in the *Hávamál* and also in Snorri's tale: *Skáldskaparmál*. In fact, the latter makes sense of the disparate nature of the former.

Historically, they can both be sourced in much older pictographic images recorded in stone some four centuries prior to Snorri's garbled but vital summations. Drawing together the mysteries of our fragmented harvest customs, 'Crying the Neck' observed during the reaping tide of 1836, is perhaps the most intriguing. Witnessed by W. Hone, it is here paraphrased as:

"An old man, goes round to the shocks and sheaves picking out a little bundle of all the best ears he can find and tying them up into a very neat bundle. This is called "the neck" of wheat, or wheaten ears. After the field is cut out, the reapers and binders, stand round in a circle. The person with "the neck" stands in the centre grasping it with both hands. After some swaying and chanting the 'neck' is thrown up by the maker in the centre of the circle of reapers, who all clamour for the neck, whilst turning their own from it, lest they be seen catching it.

After having thus repeated "the neck" three times, and "wee yen" or "way yen" likewise, they break into laughter, great mirth and raucous capering's, flinging their hats into the air. The one who gets the "neck" must run hard and fast up to the farm-house where the dairy-maid stands prepared with a pail of water in one hand and a jug of cider in the other. The winner of 'the neck' must gain entry to the house, by any means, but must be unseen; if he achieves this, he is kissed by the maid and is lauded with cider. If not he is drenched with water and scooted out of the house."

Clearly the parallels between this tale and Óðinn's are indisputable: the reapers encircling the old man, the cry, the jostle for the neck, the reward sought by gainful entry into the premises in which the maid hides, holding the vessel (of cider in this case), he woes the girl, is kissed and receives the pitcher of cider (known in the Craft as: 'the

Harvest–tide Supper [33]

33. Pieter Bruegel the Elder- *'The Harvesters.'* Public Domain, Wiki Commons License.

water of the wise' – the wisdom ale of the ancestors). The cup raised in lieu of mead is offered in thanks for a good harvest understood as partaking of:

"The essence of experience, or juice of judgement, likened to a fermentation from that fruit which grew upon the tree of knowledge; this is what we really harvest from our human lives on earth, and that is why we have chosen an apple-ale to consume with our feast...)."

Cider has long been a traditional beverage with which to toast a successful harvest. During the harvest suppers, set amongst the 'groaning table', sometimes the 'neck' would be placed at the head of the table as a mark of respect throughout the reverential and conversely, bawdy celebrations afterwards.

Subject to varied and speculative theories, the origins of this strange pagan tradition – 'Crying the Neck' is all too frequently dismissed as too remote to properly ascertain. And yet, despite the time lag, its particular signatory presence remains an honoured custom celebrating the manifold mysteries of our harvest customs.

Though ere so long distant in the annals of history, that now, only their echoes remain to tease us, we may yet partake from it a gleaning of its truth. But first we need to seek that knowledge within ancestral memory of families who lived and worked the land. Theirs was an era that recalled those songs, faint traces whispered upon the winds, where country folk still understood the lore pertaining to the sacrificial elements that pervaded the conclusion of the harvest.

Despite their garbled histories, it is not unreasonable to assume a probable cohesion at source linking the deaths of the Nine fabled Reapers noted in Óðinn's artful acquisition of the mead, to the nine deaths attributed to the nonogrammatic sacrificial feast – the *'Disting/Disablot'*

Dísablót

held at Uppsala in Sweden every nine years[34] (eight actual years by lunar count[35])

Looking now towards the prize, the bundle of wheat called – the 'neck,' it is perhaps best expressed as the 'spirit

---

34. Nine stones, blessed eight! The necklace/girdle yet again features. 8 of course relates to Venus as well as the moon   35. http://www.astro.uu.se/archast/Henriksson.pdf
Image: – by Malmstrom Public Domain, Wiki Commons License

of the corn;' the virtue of life held by the one who wields the whetstone's authority. Thus, having the power of life over death, knowledge over ignorance and poetry over prose, truly we perceive the virtue of the gods as eternal for man alone lives and dies.

And so, derived from the Old Norse phrase for a 'sheaf of corn' the 'neck' clearly becomes the vehicle for that virtue in seed and as a medium of fermentation; euphemisms in fact, for blood and bone. Preserved within our rich store of northern folktales (for whom we owe thanks to the mammoth efforts of literary giants Jacob Grimm et al), we can retrieve snippets of lore that coalesce all disparate pieces within this arcane puzzle. Each weaves

The Yule Boar [36]

36. *'Bringing in the Boar's Head.'* 1873. Public Domain, Wiki Commons License.

one into another, seamlessly, threading the lives of all who speak and hear them together again, removed from time and place. Shifting along the tide a bit further, we drift into the deeper realms of life and its great round to encounter the season of contradiction; that of death in life.

But all exists within the natural cycle, and if the Mill doth not churn, then the cauldron becomes still, a thing it can never become. And so the great wheel grinds on. Around Yuletide, small cakes in honour of Freyja were baked in the shape of a boar. As this particular beast is sacred to Her, it is lauded in this darkest of all months.

The 'Yule Boar' consumed at the great Midwinter Feast is served with the apple of Iðunna within its jaw; for life given up to the Mill [Yule could mean wheel], is first honoured with its final meal. This meal is none other than the pouch of grain or 'neck' won at the harvest's end.[37]

"The boar, the stag, the ram we become, for hunter and hunted are but One!"

The warrior's portion is preserved and fed to the ploughman who eats of it, but who also ploughs the remains into the corners of the first furrows carved into the frozen ground during the New Year's Plough Monday Rite (the *Æcerbot*) following the cessation of festivities concluded at Twelfth Night.

"MAGICAL VISION, in which the participant undertakes by

---

37. It is also known how today in certain hunting circles that any animal killed is given bread, the grains of life, for its soul's journey forward. This final meal honours the life given, consumed in gyfu. Ref: 'The Hunter's Tale by Cunning Man, #60 *Hedge Wytch* All Hallows 2012.

inference part of a Triad of service, and therefore contacts certain levels.* ...to clarify this statement I ask the interested reader to examine the Hebrew letters IHVH as they would be in their original and matriarchal form, which will explain something of the basic nature of magical rite and ritual. It should be as clear as the Roebuck in the Thicket now." [38]

Roebuck hunting with Hounds [39]

'*Æcerbot*' is an 11th century magical charm that heralds the second of three major annual Blots, held by the Northern Peoples. Attested within this potent folkloric medieval charm, the Æcerbot [40]('field-remedy') is thrice invoked to an enigmatic female deity whose suggested form is probably Nerthus.

38. Roy Bowers 39. *Livre de Chasse of Gaston Phoebus*' Public Domain, Wiki Commons License . 40. Etymology for erce ...*Erce, erce, erce eorþan modor*

"The goddess feeds us, as a mother does – so in this aspect she is bountiful nature, mother earth, feeding her children, in the same way a mother does...

As the invocation currently stands in its much tattered form of erce, erce, erce, we cannot fail to notice the historical comparison to the Latin sanctus, sanctus, sanctus – for 'holy, indicating a status of extreme sacredness.'

Demeter Ceres [41]

It is an interpretation that posits a strong origin sourced in eorcnan meaning: true, genuine; holy. It also manifests in the proper name Erce, (from an earlier) or **Eorce** (EOSTER) for the potency and virtue of fertility envisioned later by some as a goddess and addressed as 'Earth Mother'.

*"Nature **Is**, and whatever Man is, so is Nature, since Man and Nature, like Beast and Nature, are one and the same thing......"*

41. Woodcut engraving from the book *"Der Olymp oder die Mythologie der Griechen und Römer (The Olympus or the Mythology of the Greeks and Romans)"*, published by August Heinrich Petiscus in C.F. Amelang's Verlag, Leipzig (1878, 18th edition). Public Domain, Wiki Commons License.

Unsurprisingly, the 19th century scholar of northern traditions, Jacob Grimm, similarly identified Nerthus as the Germanic earth-mother who appeared under such names as Erda, Erce, Fru Gaue, Fjörgyn, Frau Holda and Hluodana. Grimm also noted the Old High German erchan meaning 'genuine, true or (magic) hallowed!

"All known relationships and many unknown ones are to be found in natural laws. The supernatural never comes into it..."

It can surely be no coincidence that *cere* equates with IHVH in letter sequence too. Note also similarity to keres – greek for cereal and for *Keres* the Greek goddess of agriculture.

The Æcerbot ritual is arduous, taking a whole day, with prayers and chants repeated in various stages, namely the four corners of the field. The previous eve announces the beginning when clods of earth are carefully removed from each of the corners and brought into the centre. Here they

Anglo-Saxon Ploughmen

Image: [Facsimile of a Miniature in a mediaeval manuscript published by Shaw, with legend "*God Spede þe plough, and send us korne enow.*" Note that "þe" should be transliterated "the". Project Gutenberg text 10940 Title: *Manners, Custom and Dress During the Middle Ages and During the Renaissance Period* Public Domain, Wiki Commons License.

are mixed with a paste made from honey, milk, yeast, oil and vibrant pungent healthy herbage (so long as it is not leguminous).

Although the rite at this time is fully Christianised, the sods were taken to mass, to be blessed with the sign of the cross before they were replanted before nightfall. And so, with poultice in hand, the ploughman would face east, await the dawn and turn three times Sun-wise, lauding the earth goddess Nerthus:

"Erce, erce, erce eorþan modor, mother of earth".

The field was then ploughed with a chant hailing "earth, mother of mortals." Though Christianised, the form of this would typically reflect and maintain elements of the early pagan prayer. The Call to the Earth Mother slowly became replaced with a prayer to the trinity with a particular plea to Mary to make the earth fertile once again. Considerable speculation surrounds this archaic call, and Grimm was perhaps the closest in his association of 'erce' with the Old High German erchan [perchen] for the 'True One, the Mother, the origin of all:' *Dame Percha, Bertha, ertha, erce.*

Of especial note is the more than coincidental link between Urdhr and Ertha which is too close to allow it to pass without further comment. Within the context of this ritual, calling upon Her for a kinder fate would certainly not be an unreasonable summation.

It is noted by the keen observances of Tacitus, how the 'Angli' peoples were clearly goddess worshipers, who considered the earth as their mother. The name Nerthus is generally held to be a Latinized form of Proto-Germanic *Nerþuz*, which is the Proto-Germanic precursor to the Old Norse deity name *Njörðr*, who is a male deity in works recorded in the 13th century. Various scholarly theories exist regarding the goddess and her potential later traces amongst the Germanic peoples.

INVOKATION TO EARTH

"I do conjure thee, Earth
Now in the secret hour of night
Ebb and flow meeting
And as for my place, precisely stand centred
By this, the mystery of my Craft
Entrenched I see the boundary round
And of ought else, nought but the riding moon,
And these possess my thought and soul
Facing my truth to them
For I desire no other thought but these
For since long time I do require to learn
The truth of truths
Yea verily have I suffered to achieve
The life becoming spirit
And know that good and evil will prevail
Within no forced equality
Circle and moon be gracious to me." [42]

---

42. This invocation by Roy Bowers, is accompanied by a prayer to the 'Farmer' as the Lord of this World.

By contrast, the Langobardi – though few and surrounded by mighty nations – were fierce and bold. They are known best for their passionate worship of Nerthus – the Earth Mother. They demonstrated a belief that she interests herself in human affairs, traveling amongst her people in disguise, much as did Demeter, in search of Persephone.

Upon a sacred Island a sacred grove housed a consecrated cart, draped with cloth, which none but the priest could touch. Once the priest perceives 'Her' presence within the cart - the holy of holies, he would attend Her in deepest reverence as her cart, drawn by heifers, circumambulates the towns dedicated to Her.

"There are as many ways of seeing god as there are creations of god, and each individual creation is the totality, the hand that writes and the writing.."[43]

Days of rejoicing and merry-making follow in Her wake. No one may draw arms in Her presence and all such must be hidden. After that the cart, the cloth and, if you care to believe it, the 'goddess' herself are bathed in seclusion within the holy waters of Nerthus. Performed by slaves who afterwards drown in the lake it is a tale of 'awe-ful' reverence.

"Where nature ultimately fails is that nature is illusion as we see nature, but not as nature really is…all mystical perception is based upon the fact that we go to god, not that god comes to us."[44]

43. Roy Bowers. 44. Roy Bowers

And Madame Guiden Corn can be found sourced in these early Teutonic terms

- GUD, GUDE, s. used for the name of God, S.(traced to gothic) bonus/bounty
- GUDE, GUID, GOOD, GUDIN v. a. To manure
- GUIDON/GUIDEN, s. A standard. (Fr.)
- Gode/Gaud/Gaude: GOUD, s. Gold, S. Teut.:

Etymology: yAthArthya = Sanskrit for Truth

Despite the clarity of meaning in this short digression, we have determined with impunity the reverence of and for the very earth, whose corporeality is at all times imbued with the Preternatural. Her shining presence, Her virtue where gifted, becomes as precious as gold and as vital as food. In fact absence is inimical for mind and body.

Now we must continue our exploration into the contextual landscape of myth and ritual, poetry and magic; being sure to emphasise the incredible beauty and acceptance of those things we might consider today the less than palatable elements of our humanity and of life itself. A harsh life induces both despair and desire. Together, these bring forth poetic vision within the very pragmatisms typified by such extreme and random states of existence.

Special as the 'acerbot' ritual is, we must elucidate 'truc' significance to that mystery within. It must present even beyond the theatrics and the expressive dependency upon the fructifying earth, the true value and merit of this hoary enterprise.

Roy Bowers was keen to note how:

Madame le Guiden [45]

45. Anselm Feuerbach *Gaea*. 1875. Public Domain, Wiki Commons License.

"It is said by various "authorities" that the Faith of the Wise, when they do believe in its existence, is a simple matter: a pre-Christian religion based upon whatever Gods and Goddesses are the current vogue--full of simple, hearty peasants doing simple, hearty peasant-like things ... things that in some cases complex, nervous sophisticates also enjoy doing in urban parlours...All this worries me somewhat – since I am not a peasant and neither am I particularly interested in being led by a sweet woman, and ritual to me is merely a means to an end.

So what is the Faith all about? Admittedly I can only speak for myself, and what I write here are my own opinions, but here goes.

The Loving Cup[46]

46. Dante Gabriel Rossetti – *The Loving Cup* 1867. Public Domain, Wiki Commons License. 47. *The Faith of the Wise* by Robert Cochrane *Pentagram* (4) August 1965

Unfortunately for authorities, students and "mere seekers after truth," the Faith is not about anything that has been written above. The Faith is finally concerned with Truth, total Truth. It is one of the oldest of religions, and also one of the most potent, bringing as it does, Man into contact with Gods, and Man into contact with Self. As such the Faith is a way of life different and distinct from any theory promulgated by the authorities or historians.

Within the disciplines of the Faith, man may offer devotion to the Gods, and receive certain knowledge of Their existence by participation in something of the perfected Nature of Godhead, recalling that both within and without which is most true. The Faith is a belief concerned with the inner nature of devotion, and finally with the nature of mysticism and mystical experience. I

It has, in common with all great religions, an inner experience that is greater than the exterior world. It is a discipline that creates from the world an enriched inward vision. It can and does embrace the totality of human experience from birth to death, then beyond."[47]

And again in:

"According to further information it is a traditional religion based upon an exceedingly simplified concept of the works of Nature. It is by inference from their rituals as reported, an attempt to bribe Nature by various actions and beliefs into a malleable state,......There has been no cause for a fertility religion in Europe since the advent of the coulter-share plough in the thirteenth century, the discovery of haymaking, selective breeding of animals, etc. To claim, as some witches do, that there is a greater need in the world for fertility of mind than before is understating general facts, since Western Europe

---

47. The Faith of the Wise by Robert Cochrane *Pentagram* (4) August 1965

morally and socially has advanced more without the Old Craft and its attendant superstitions than it ever did with them. The value of the Old Craft today is that in it lie the seeds of the Old Mystery tradition. Through this the witch may perceive the beginnings of that ultimate in wisdom, knowledge of themselves and of their motives. The genuine Mysteries are open to all, because anyone having experience enough can understand that basic Message."[48]

And finally:

"Therefore it can be shown that the Faith is a complex philosophy, dealing finally with the nature of Truth, Experience and Devotion. It requires discipline and work; plus utter and complete devotion to the common aim. It can only be fulfilled by service, some labours taking many years to complete. The Faith tolerates no nonsense, and those who would come to it, must come empty-handed saying "I know nothing, I seek everything," since within the structure of the Faith, all things may be contained and are contained. ... It is nearly impossible to enter unless the supplicant shows unmistakable signs of past memory and a genuine mystical drive, and is willing to undertake tests that will force him finally to disclose that matter which is most secret to himself. The Faith has no secrets in the sense that there are formulas which can be readily understood and taught. It is finally and utterly the True Faith, standing immovable beyond space, time and all human matters."[49]

And so the true context for all such historical rites as something to both remember and take note of in ways that

---

48. *The Craft Today* by Robert Cochrane *Pentagram* (2) November 1964. 49. *The Faith of the Wise* by Robert Cochrane in Pentagram (4) August 1965 – Public Domain

The Dancing Floor [50]

we may evolve within the Craft is utterly unambiguous. In viewing again the occasion in 1930 when the last authentic 'Crying of the Neck' ceremony held in like manner of the same traditional rite as relayed above by Hone, almost a hundred years earlier in 1836, we may begin to see a glimmer of that oblique mystery.

50. Detail from *Procession and Dance of the Nymphs* by Wilhelm Volz, 1898. Public Domain, Wiki Commons License

After the horrors of the world wars and the deprivations in their wake ceased and eased, the country slowly turned again, somewhat nostalgically to another time, giving freedoms for revivalists to raise again the banners of a heritage so faint in memory yet so deeply ingrained.

For their sake alone do we now celebrate a glorious plethora of many regional variations on this vital theme. All retain a tenacious fragment of the original, intrinsic to the tale, steeped in fundamental clues of both origin and true significance that serve to enrich our continued understanding and disclosure of these remarkable customs.

Further research into this vast reservoir of harvest lore, past and present that may shed further light on these intriguing mysteries is duty bound to bring forth the infamous tale of 'John Barleycorn,' the lynch-pin of all folk tradition. In recent years some scholars have recognised a link between the quasi historical hero in the Anglo-Saxon mythical epic Beowulf and the etymology of his name, which is, coincidently –'barley' (Sceaf, Ing, the sheaf, the seed, life, death and all sacrifice to itself in a perpetual cycle).

The song celebrates the suffering and sacrifice of (Beowulf as) John Barleycorn noting his resurrection through the edifying tonic his spilled blood generates.

"RELIGIOUS VISION, in which the worshipper is allowed admission to the True Godhead for a short time. This is a part of true initiation, and the results of devotion towards a mystical aim."[51]

51. Roy Bowers

The folklore surrounding this tale of death and resurrection addresses the cycle of life, particularly of the seed, harvested, reaped, and replanted in the fertilised ground, for the succour of all genera to come. On a deeper, more ancestral level, the verses yield great wisdom as memory and knowledge, hindsight and foresight, the two mainstays of Oðhin, his blessed gift to humanity through the 'Mead of Poetry.'

An early English version runs thusly

JOHN BARLEYCORN (MUST DIE)

*"There were three men came **out of the west**,*
their fortunes for to try
And these three men made a solemn vow,
John Barleycorn must die
They've ploughed, they've sown,
they've harrowed him in
Threw clods upon his head
And these three men made a solemn vow,
John Barleycorn was dead
They've let him lie for a very long time,
'til the rains from heaven did fall
And little Sir John sprung up his head
and so amazed them all.
They've let him stand 'til Midsummer's Day,'
til he looked both pale and wan.
And little Sir John's grown a long long beard,
and so become a man.

They've hired men with their scythes so sharp to cut him off
at the knee. They've rolled him and tied him
by the way, serving him most barbarously.
They've hired men with their sharp pitchforks who've pricked him to
the heart.
And the loader he has served him worse than that.
*For **he's bound him to the cart.***
They've wheeled him around and around a field
'til they came onto a pond
And there they made a solemn oath on poor John Barleycorn [52]
They've hired men with their crabtree sticks to cut him
skin from bone
*And the **miller he has served him worse than that,***
For he's ground him between two stones.
And little Sir John and the nut brown bowl,
and his brandy in the glass
And little Sir John and the nut brown bowl
proved the strongest man at last
The huntsman he can't hunt the fox
nor so loudly to blow his horn
And the tinker he can't mend kettle or pots
without a little barleycorn"

He lives on as Beowulf in legend and now as John Barleycorn in folklore. Even the popular version by Robbie Burns' retains the death and sacrificial elements despite his cynical undertones that renders the tale without just cause;

---

52. This verse is very reminiscent of the tale recited by Tacitus of the wagon of Nerthus, taken by the priest to the sacred pool once a year.

Death of the Green [53]

JOHN BARLEYCORN: A BALLAD
BY ROBBIE BURNS 1782

"And they hae taen his very heart's blood, and drank it round and round; And still the more and more they drank, their joy did more abound. John Barleycorn was a hero bold, of noble enterprise; for if you do but taste his blood, 'twill make your courage rise.

Even so, despite the rueful wael and woe of some versions, Burns' included, they all celebrate the vivifying soma of blood transformed, given as sacrifice and consumed for the benefit of all. Such remnants remain

---

53. Simon Garbutt – Public Domain. Devon Gravestone

unerring in their steadfast graft of the historical origins suggested in Hone's witness of the later 19th-Century 'Crying the Neck 'custom and its all-important parallel in the Norse tale of how Óðinn won (back) the mead reflected in the Morris game, of Reapers Nine.

"MYSTICAL VISION, in which the servant enters into divine union with the Godhead. This state has no form, being a point where force alone is present. These are proofs, since having enjoined with such forces, there cannot afterwards be any doubts as to the nature of the experience. Man suffers from doubt at all times, but to the participant in such experience, the doubt centres around the reality of the external world, not the inner. The reality of such experience illuminates the whole life."[54]

The threads are woven, the warp and weft have seen the shuttle cross many times in this tale, and now as it reaches the final bindings, we highlight the afore mentioned Mill, in folktale and song hailed as the Mill dance or Morris game. Played across the ancient world in various forms since c1460BCE, by Roman soldiers to Middle-Eastern officials, it became extremely popular during the early medieval period across Europe, finding particular favour in medieval England amongst the priesthoods of these Blessed Isles. At Westminster Abbey, Canterbury, Gloucester, Norwich, Salisbury Cathedrals several carved and drilled boards have been authenticated, set into cloister seats to accommodate this popular game.

Shakespeare's writings attest to the familiarity of the

54. Roy Bowers

Woodwose[55]

game and the dance in his era was immortalised in '*A Midsummer Night's Dream*' within which Titania refers disappointedly to an area within the woodland known as the "*The Nine Men's Morris is filled up with mud*" after devastation from the summer rains. Similarly, the origins of the word 'Morris' remain largely speculative where at least one academic asserts a possible source in the Latin word '*merellus*,' referring to a counter or gaming piece of

55. Martin Schongauer engraving, *Shield with a Greyhound*, 1480s. Public Domain, Wiki Commons License.

great antiquity.

The Nine Men's Morris board's design composed of *three concentric squares* with several transversal lines contrives the all-important and highly significant *24 points of intersection or nodes*. Two players are each provided with *nine counters, one set black, and one set white,* laid strategically upon certain points, the object being to get three in a row (a Mill) representing the Fates perhaps? Certainly this stylized format has formed the basis for numerous dances, adapted in many ways since in accord to the natural evolution of custom and the vagaries of tradition. To the early medieval Celtic language Tribes and Clans of the Northern regions, the symbolic lines and nodes were deemed to exert a sacred protective function.

Additionally, the Morris Square itself represented the

Sacred Mounds [56]

56. *The Mounds in Gamla Uppsala* 1840. Public Domain, Wiki Commons License.

Holy Omphalos, the Mother Mound or Cauldron, reached by treading the (cosmic) '*Mill*', another name for the game. It thus became a rite of seasonal regeneration, celebrated throughout the four compass directions that radiated out from the centre point, in strict adherence with the four sacred elements and the four cardinal winds.

It is, in 'Faith', '*The Castle that Spins Without Motion, 'upon the Tree of Nine Worlds fashioned*'. Intriguingly, one such board game, of Nine Men's Morris, was found in the *western mound* of the *three* royal grave mounds at Uppsala.

A most worthy conclusion would be to assign these clearly defined visionary aspects of 'the mead of poetry' as outlined with sombre prevalence in this meander through our peculiarly 'English' customs, which cumulatively express the '*Round of Life*.'

Its five stages are vividly noted by Robin-the-Dart, E. J. Jones and by Roy Bowers, celebrated collectively in the 'field of man.'

It continues to inspire all who sup from Her cornucopia within the '*field of dreams*'....
Drink heartily from the draft of wisdom – The Valorhorn of Mead issues forth!

THE NINE KNOTS

*"In the past, the male and female clans were separated
except for the Nine Rites or 'Knots' of the Year when they
came together and worshipped Godhead."*
ROBERT COCHRANE

Nine times a year, the dark of night is pierced by
the light of fires kindled by the People; those who
continue to cultivate the ancient inspirations and traditional
way of doing things mediated and handed on by Robert
Cochrane. The Rites are observed at times and dates long
held sacred, and indeed the Clan's ritual calendar would
be familiar to those informed by ecclesiastical liturgy, or
Gerald Gardner's Wicca and various neo-pagan traditions
that adopted or adapted his Wheel of the Year.

Clan Maid Shani Oates writes:

*"The Clan of Tubal Cain celebrate nine special occasions through
the year as follows: Yule, Twelfth Night (Wild Hunt), Candlemas,
Lady Day, May's Eve (Roodmas), Midsummer, Feast of Hekate,
Michaelmas and All Hallows (Martinmas), that honour ancestral
traditions drawn from across Europe and the more ancient Middle*

East… Evolved seasonal celebrations honour the 'Wheel of Fate'… as a cosmological encryption regarding cycles of birth, death, fate within our unique heritage." [57]

Here, the human experience played out upon the surface of the earth reflects the apparent motion of the constellations of heaven.

THE STAR THAT LEADS THE WAY

"'Look, you have been told everything. Lift up your eyes and look at the cloud and the light within it and the stars surrounding it. The star that leads the way is your star.' Judas lifted up his eyes and saw the luminous cloud, and he entered it." [58]

A day in the life of a man or woman, from waking to sleep, reflects the lifetime of man and woman, from birth to death; and human life reflects, in turn, the greater drama of life on earth – that all must change and know decay. Through the myths and mysteries of the Nine Knots, the People perceive themselves within Fate, their origin, their destiny, the reality of their being.

"Magic and religion are aids to overcome Fate…" [59]

The cycles of life on earth, then reflect evolutionary cycles of the cosmos, from Genesis to the Apocalypse, or from the meeting of fire and frost in the Ginnungagap to the Ragnarok – and beyond.

57. Oates, S. 2010 *Tubelo's Green Fire* Mandrake of Oxford UK p42 58. Kasser, R; Meyer, M; Wurst, G (eds) *The Gospel of Judas* pp. 43-44 National Geographic USA
59. Robert Cochrane: *The Robert Cochrane Letters: The Star-Crossed Serpent III*, Shani Oates (Ed) 2016 Mandrake of Oxford.

Sacred Fire as Destruction[60]

60. *Fire*, by Giuseppe Arcimboldo, 1572. Public Domain, Wiki Commons License.

We see here in action the hermetic maxim:

"*As above, so below.*"

This may even be seen in the fire that burns within the compass on those nine nights. Appropriately hallowed, the flames that consume the wood make visible the cunning fire, and the blaze of forge, hearth, and altar.

CAIN THE WANDERER

"*We have the spirit of Cain or Abel within us, the seeker or the sleeper...*"[61]

Each fire kindled on those nights shines like a star in darkest night; seen together, they form on earth a detailed representation of heavenly bodies and constellations of importance within Clan mythos – heavenly bodies and constellations that are themselves icons of Clan ancestors and deities, Cain among them.

"*As Boötes, the 'farmer' Cain rises, fecunds the Earth; the harvest is reaped, Cain dies. [The myth] reveals Cain as the original and eternal progenitor, relating in fact the concept of palingenesis where the cosmic cycle of deification, expressed through the old god as the 'Father' dies, and the new god, his son or younger version of himself is reborn. It is one of sacrifice, dispersal, and re-union within itself.*"[62]

The myth of the Farmer, who, as Harvester/Slayer of the Shepherd is also warrior-king and sacrificing priest, and who begat the Smith, is played out in the night sky

61.Shani Oates – Oates, S. 2012 *The Star Crossed Serpent Volume* II p 139 Mandrake of Oxford UK   62. Shani Oates – Oates, S. 2012 *The Star Crossed Serpent Volume* II p 129 Mandrake of Oxford UK.

and mirrored in the Star Compass. His tale calls to mind Masculine Mysteries and their evolutionary virtues of learning, teaching, skill, bravery, and truthfulness, taught by Woman according to our Clan Mythos.[63]

His starry myth is told and re-told, witnessed and witnessed again; night's ebon void and earth's dark horizon both stage and backdrop. His story takes place within the wide, slow curves of the cosmic cycles of life and death, coagulation and dissolution. The stellar wanderings of the Farmer, whom we could think of as a 'celestial avatar,' distant and remote from the earth, become something of a pattern or blueprint for the Smith, the 'earthly avatar' and 'descendant' of the Farmer.[64]

Glimpsing the moon but briefly, it shows Cain as the

Stellar Maiden[65]

63 Ibid.   64. See Robin-the-Dart's *Cain: an agricultural myth?* republished in Oates, S. 2012 *The Star Crossed Serpent Volume II* pp. 129–133 Mandrake of Oxford UK   65. *Magnæ Deorum Matris* by Athanasius Kircher (1602–1680). Public Domain, Wiki Commons License.

Man in the Moon, and reveals Saturn as Father of Time and Death, and KephRe, the backside of the sun (the lesser light)[66]. The blood is the life, and the People, bonded and bound by blood, trace their lineage back to Tubal Cain, and, through him, to the Shining One, Son of the Morning Star, and lux mundi, the light of the world.

AVE MARIS STELLA

"One of the deepest and most appealing images in the Faith is that of the Virgin and Child…"

Laid upon the Nine Knots, Cain of the Star-Compass appears as a dominant, male figure. This is not to the detriment or diminishment of Herself. This becomes more apparent when we look beyond the fixed stars of Cain's sign to other constellations significant to this strand of Clan mythology, such as Draco, and to the dark depths in which shine the moon and the stars. Within the Star-Compass, as Draco, she appears at Lammastide as the Muse and as the Great Initiatrix[67].

However, Boötes/Cain and the other relevant heavenly bodies are contained within the night sky, the darkness of which paradoxically reveals Herself as Fate, the three cosmic Mothers and weavers of past, present, and future, in which the avatar makes his archetypal journey. She may also be discerned in Sabbat skies as Hekate the torch-bearer and star-maiden daughter of Nyx, Inanna the bright Queen of Heaven, mother Frigg with Her distaff, and Mary who is both

66. Cf. Oates, S. 2010 Tubelo's Green Fire p 48 Mandrake of Oxford UK 67. See Robin-the-Dart's *Cain: an agricultural myth?* republished in Oates, S. 2012 *The Star Crossed Serpent Volume II* pp. 129 –133 Mandrake of Oxford UK

Stella maris, star of the sea, and Stella matutina, the Morning Star whose glittering appearance announces the imminent arrival of the Daystar.

The Moon points to Her as Maid, the Wise and Compassionate Mother and (also the) Compassionate/Wise Woman — a reflection of the Ambivalent and Compassionate Goddess who is white with works of good, and black with works of darkness.[68] The bright, shining white Goddess is also the Pale-Faced goddess of death; the black goddess, dark yet lovely[69].

As Cain makes his way through starry night, he encounters Her in Her different guises and roles as Virgin,

Phosphoros[70]

68. See *The Robert Cochrane Letters: The Star-Crossed Serpent III*, Shani Oates (Ed) 2016 Mandrake of Oxford. 69. Cf. *The Song of Solomon* 1:5 70. *Phosphoros, Eos, Helios, Hesperos.*' by Stanisław Wyspianski 1897. Public Domain, Wiki Commons License

Mother, Initiatrix, and Death Hag. In the various myths and folklore associated with the Nine Knots, She is also present as Maiden, Mother, Hierodule, Initiatrix, Crone, and Enchantress; She is Woman, and hers are the:

"Mysteries of the slow tides of creation and destruction... expressed in the pentagram, and taught by Man – Life/Birth, Love, Maternity, Wisdom, and Death/Resurrection[71].

SUN OF THE MORNING, SON OF THE MORNING STAR
The Farmer, 'born of Her', learns and perfects his skills, labours and toils, embarks upon the hero's journey, and undergoes sacrifice, dispersal and re-union[72], inspired and presided over by Her.

"Fate is a cradle that rocks the infant spirit." [73]

A third Person discerned in the skies under which the People observe the rites of the Nine Knots is Tubal Cain, grandson of Cain, and the Clan's tutelary deity. As Smith and as 'Son of the Farmer', he is 'hidden within' Boötes. Seen within the mythos of the People as an incarnate avatar, he is a fiery Prophet, and the Voice of the Father, conveying the Word, and advancing the arts of civilisation. Here, we may also see Hermes, son of Zeus, and messenger of the Gods. He is also the Shining One, Bringer of the Light of Dawn[74], whose advent is made known by the appearance

71. *The Robert Cochrane Letters: The Star-Crossed Serpent III*, Shani Oates (Ed) 2016 Mandrake of Oxford. 72. Cf. Oates, S. 2012 *The Star Crossed Serpent Volume II* p 129 Mandrake of Oxford UK 73. Robert Cochrane 74. Cf. Oates, S. 2011 *The Arcane Veil* pp. 112 - 148

Gnostic Light

Image: Frontispiece of Athanasius Kircher's book *Ars magna lucis et umbrae* I [in decem libros digesta. Quibus admirandae lucis et umbrae in mundo, atque adeo universa natura. (Rome, Scheus, 1646).] Artist unknown. Public Domain, Wiki Commons License.

of the Morning Star (Venus), and whose heavenly icon, the Sun, then rises slowly to fill our skies with golden light. As Child of the Mother, he is the Priest of the True Faith, and his are the Priestly Mysteries.

"Sophia is celestial bride of the Sun/son (who bears the triple crown)..." [75]

GNOSTIC LIGHT

These can be seen as the "offspring" of the coming together of the Male and Female Mysteries, and can be discerned within Cochrane's five proofs required by devotion, which he:

"Stressed as empathic realisations borne of direct and unequivocal visionary contact" [76],

and that *"demonstrate the evolution of: perception, gnosis, seership, vigil (challenge/trial/surrender) and union (Individuation)."* [77]

As celestial groom of Sophia, he bears the triple-crown, and leads and serves his People as their King. The four stations mark the midpoints and furthermost points (equinoxes and solstices) of the Sun's apparent motion through the sky, and could be seen as a solar version of the myth of Cain as seen in the Star-Compass[78]. In other words, Tubal Cain, as the solar, younger aspect of the stellar father Cain, also walks the path of sacrifice, dispersal and re-union. As sailors and other travellers navigate by the sun, so may

75. Shani Oates – Oates, S. 2010 *Tubelo's Green Fire* p 164 Mandrake of Oxford UK 76. Cf. Oates, S 2012 *The Star Crossed Serpent Volume II* p 64 Mandrake of Oxford UK 77. Ibid. 78. See Robin-the-Dart's Cain: an agricultural myth? republished in Oates, S. 2012 *The Star Crossed Serpent Volume II* pp. 129–133 Mandrake of Oxford UK

the People, collectively and individually, navigate their way through their own participation in the journey as plotted out by Cain in the Star-Compass.

"Bring forth the Star-Son..." [79]

ANCHORING THE HEAVENS TO THE EARTH

"In fact it is by [the solstices and equinoxes] and other seasonal markers that the stars may be observed, anchoring the Heavens to the Earth within the Compass. Annual narratives relating legend, myth and folk history are dramatized still, through which unfold the themes of creation, existence and evolution in synchronicity with the motion of the stars and the seasons. They are living myths..." [80]

Heroic Dual [81]

79. *The Robert Cochrane Letters: The Star-Crossed Serpent III*, Shani Oates (Ed) 2016 Mandrake of Oxford. 80. Shani Oates 2012 *The Star Crossed Serpent Volume II* p128 Mandrake of Oxford UK   81. Hans Burgkmair I, '*The Fight in the Forest*,' c.1500 – 1503 Public Domain, Wiki Commons License.

The Heavens are anchored to the Earth within, and beyond, the compass on the Nine Knots, in rites whereby the People, duly prepared, raise forces 'by prayer and faith', until

"Something of Godhead's finally revealed, and that which is within and without is partially understood".[82]

Boötes/Cain, or another constellation that symbolises the Clan's overarching myth offers the foundation, a traditional way of doing things, upon which further structures are built; putting flesh on the bones, as it were. Form for the forces raised is provided for within and without.

HEROIC DUAL

The People prepare themselves as outer form for force by preparing inner form through fasting, prayer, and the study of, and reflection and meditation upon, key themes and concepts within non-corporeal correspondences, folklore mythologies, seasonal rituals, and various other praxes, particular to the Knot being hallowed. The scope is enormous. Like wheels within wheels, various strands of Clan mythos, and Male, Female, and Priestly Mysteries may be laid upon the ring of the Knots.

Fleshed out through further study, prayer, and contemplation, this further nuances the inner forms created by individuals. One might engage themes of learning, life/birth, and perception at Yule; teaching, love, and gnosis

82. Cochrane, R 1965 *The Faith of the Wise* http://www.clanoftubalcain.org.uk/the_letters/FOTW_article_lk.pdf

at Candlemas; skill, maternity, and seer-ship at Lady Day; or one might engage those same themes from Candlemas (emergence from the Mound) onwards.

Or one might apply them only to the 'Great Sabbats,' and allow the Knots of the equinoxes and solstices to 'shed more light' on those themes. Working sites and areas, tools such as the Stang, garlands, seasonal decorations and foods and other corporeal correspondences announce the mythic and other themes of the relevant Knot, and also provide outer form. The People gather on the vigil of each festival, inflame themselves by prayer, receive holy viaticum, and shift themselves from the land of the quick to the realms of the gods. Perception is increased in hope of Divine revelation which brings understanding and gnosis.

"Comprehended in the physical person of the participant until it becomes one with his total being. The forces comprehended are part of the living person, [and are] incorporated into everyday life as part of a spiritual, mental and physical discipline that returns the devotee again and again to the original Source" [83]

The Knots, then, are not gaudy pantomimes and sympathetic magics, half-read from tattered scripts, to ensure the sun comes up the next morning. They are, instead, the means by which the People align and re-align themselves with the potencies that shine within their totemic stars, being and becoming avatars, channels of

83. Cochrane, R. 1965 *The Faith of the Wise* http://www.clanoftubalcain.org.uk/ the_letters/FOTW_article_lk.pdf

Godhead on earth. They are high points and holy days of a craft that might be compared with the path of bhakti yoga, the spirit of which may be found in the honeyed words of Krishna in his 'Song of the Beloved':

"Engage your mind always in thinking of Me, become My devotee, offer obeisances to Me and worship Me. Being completely absorbed in Me, surely you will come to Me… One can understand Me as I am, as the Supreme Personality of Godhead, only by devotional service. And when one is in full consciousness of Me by such devotion, he can enter into the kingdom of God."[84]

The Nine Knots are occasions of worship. For Cochrane they were (and are):

"… always about duty… to be mindful of the weight of service, and to honour the gods and live in fate… 'in the rightness of things'. This is to love one's self, and humanity, which reflects the gods upon earth."[85]

WYTCHES SABBAT

Observed mindfully, with right intention, will, humility, love, and determined determination, the myth-in-action of the rituals becomes prayer, and a key that opens ancient, ancestral ways that lead from the world, through the worlds, and into the mystical experience of Holy Communion and Her grace-filled gift of evolutionary gnosis, that, in the end, She may gather them home again.

---

84. Prabhupada, A. (Ed.) 1972 Bhagavad-gita As It Is pp. 441 and 739 Bhaktivedanta Book Trust India 85 Oates, S; Private correspondence

The Wytches' Sabbat [86]

86. *Sorceries from Astra Castra* . Artist unknown. Public Domain, Wiki Commons License.

"The Faith is… concerned with Truth, total Truth… Within the disciplines of the Faith, man may offer devotion to the Gods, and receive certain knowledge of Their existence by participation in something of the perfected nature of Godhead, recalling that both within and without which is most true."[87]

Christmas mummers dancing

A HERETIC'S CATECHESIS ON THE LITURGICAL YEAR

The diverse rites of old Europe and the Middle East found their way to 'catholic' celebration in the calendar of the church. Important dates and celebrations, and the themes, concepts, and mysteries contained within them, of various cultures were given a Christian gloss and grafted onto and into the existing calendar and rites of the Church[88], and largely still-pagan People.

Without doubt, we can be fairly sure, they were perceived heretically in existing ecclesial ceremonies, rites, and symbols echoes of their own Faith.

87. Cochrane, R. 1965 *The Faith of the Wise* http://www.clanoftubalcain.org.uk/the_letters/FOTW_article_lk.pdf 88. Cf. Oates, S. 2010 *Tubelo's Green Fire* p 43 Mandrake of Oxford UK. Image: From an engraving in an 1847 gift book from *Old England: A Pictorial Museum*: Unknown engraver. Public Domain, Wiki Commons License.

CHRISTMAS/YULE

"The people who walked in darkness have seen a great light; those who dwelt in a land of deep darkness, on them has light shined."[89]

Thought arises in the mind of Godhead; the chaos and void of Tzimtzum opens wide, and a shaft of light pierces the darkness. The light-bearing avatar, sun of the Old King, is born in the depths of Mother Night, perceived and celebrated by the Faithful, with feasting and gift-giving in temples festooned with greenery and homes decked with holly, as the birth and re-birth of the light, and all potential, within themselves, and perceive themselves as the light born in night.

"Cain again begins to arise, slowly..."[90]

TWELFTH NIGHT

"Now when Jesus was born in Bethlehem of Judea in the days of Herod the king, behold, Wise Men from the East came to Jerusalem, saying, 'Where is he who has been born king of the Jews? For we have seen his star in the East, and have come to worship him.'"[91]

In the light of hollen torches on the feast of the Epihany, the Faithful recall the Magi's quest to find the light-bearer, born in time; the search for and revelation of God within self.

The Magi's consultation with Herod sets in motion his

---

89. Isaiah 9:2 90. See Robin-the-Dart's *Cain: an agricultural myth?* republished in Oates, S. 2012 *The Star Crossed Serpent Volume II* pp. 129 - 133 Mandrake of Oxford UK 91. Matthew 2: 1-2

Holy Fire[92]

wild hunt for the new-born Sacred King, and the massacre of the Holy Innocents. The light-filled vessel emanating into Tzimtzum shatters, and the shards are crystalized and embedded. The Plough is blessed as the Quadrantids, the seeds of the Farmer, fall from the sky.

"Cain is risen!" [93]

Bootes [94]

92. Augsburger Wunderzeichenbuch, Folio 28, 1552. Public Domain, Wiki Commons License. 93. See Robin-the-Dart's *Cain: an agricultural myth?* republished in Oates, S. 2012 *The Star Crossed Serpent Volume II* pp. 129 – 133 Mandrake of Oxford UK. 94. *Boötes* – Ultima Thulean. Public Domain, Wiki Commons License

CANDLEMAS

"When the time came for their purification according to the law of Moses, the parents of Jesus brought him up to Jerusalem to present him to the Lord..." [95]

The Virgin Mother emerges from the solitude and silences of her post-partum ritual seclusion and presents the Child of Light at the Temple, where the Child is perceived by righteous Simeon as a *"light for revelation to the Gentiles"*, and where she is purified according to the law.

The Faithful undergo ritual purifications, removing inner and external obstacles that hinder progress and the apprehension of naked Truth; the Child born of the love in their hearts is reflected, in a special way, by Her living representative on earth. The Bright Goddess is perceived within the Mary of the Gael; throats are blessed with crossed candles on the feast of St Blaise; the Virgin appears at Lourdes, where She speaks words of conversion and penance to Bernadette, guides her to uncover the healing spring, and reveals Herself as the Immaculate Conception.

"Cain, now a fully risen arc emblazoned across the sky." [96]

LADY DAY

"The angel said to her, 'Do not be afraid, Mary, for you have found favour with God. And behold, you will conceive in your womb and bear a son, and you shall call his name Jesus... The Holy Spirit will come upon you and the power of the Most High will overshadow you...'" [97]

95. Luke 2: 22. 96. See Robin-the-Dart's *Cain: an agricultural myth?* republished in Oates, S. 2012 The Star Crossed Serpent Volume II pp. 129 - 133 Mandrake of Oxford UK 97 Luke 1: 30-31, 35

The Annunciation of the archangel Gabriel to the Virgin Mary, and the conception in Her womb of the light-bearing avatar, is celebrated by the Faithful with symbols of life and light, even as they recall the creation of Adam in Edenic paradise, and Eve's seduction by the Serpent that leads her to eat from the Tree of the Knowledge of Good and Evil. Inanna receives the Mè from Enki, and empowers Her King, crowning him with them in the union of Sacred Marriage. Jesus' anointing by Mary of Bethany is often recalled around this time of year, due to its link with the movable feast of Easter, in which we may perceive [the much misinterpreted act of] 'Cain slaying the Shepherd,' and reflect on the underscoring theme of sacrifice involved in incarnation and the origin and duties of divine kingship.

"Cain approaches close to optimum zenith"[98]

ROODMAS/MAY EVE

"O sacred wood! In Thee fulfill'd Was holy David's truthful lay! Which told the world, that from a tree The Lord should all the nations sway." [99]

The Faithful celebrate the Finding of the Cross, stained with blood and with water, the Tree of Life, by St Helena, and its recovery from the Persians by Heraclius.

The light-bearing avatar has bared his arm, and waxes

---

98 See Robin-the-Dart's *Cain: an agricultural myth?* republished in Oates, S. 2012 *The Star Crossed Serpent Volume II* pp. 129–133 Mandrake of Oxford UK. 99. from *Vexilla Regis* – Lefebvre, G 1959 *Saint Andrew Daily Missal* p 882-883 Liturgical Apostolate, Abbey of St Andrew Belgium

'A-Maying' [100]

100. *Queen Gwinevere* by John Collier. Public Domain, Wiki Commons License

strong, even as the realm of nature bursts forth with ever-increasing growth in the light and warmth of the summer sun. Jack in Green leads the People in the merry dance of verdant gnosis as they Beat the Bounds; the Maypole is covered in a weaving of ribbons red and white; earth and heaven are joined by the cosmic pillar, even as the branches of world tree, and those who hang upon them, stretch and unfurl upwards.

The bonfire-lit birthday celebrations of St John the Baptist, the greatest of the Old King's prophets and older cousin of the avatar, give form to the People's engagement with various mythic strands that include themes of Tannist duellists, and the relationship between Father and Son. Contemplating the birth and life of his cousin, the sacred king recognises the spirit that is embodied by St John is also within himself.

In this Holy Communion, the young king shifts into the aspect of the Old King; the Son into the aspect of the Father. The feast of the Apostles Peter and Paul, the feast of the Most Precious Blood, the Visitation of the Blessed Virgin, and St Mary Magdalene are all celebrated in the days and weeks that follow. The summer sun begins its gradual decline, and the shortening days foreshadow the ordeals, trials and initiations to be faced by the king.

"Cain begins his descent..."[101]

---

101. See Robin-the-Dart's *Cain: an agricultural myth?* republished in Oates, S. 2012 *The Star Crossed Serpent Volume II* pp. 129–133 Mandrake of Oxford UK

LAMMAS/ASSUMPTION OF THE BLESSED VIRGIN/ FEAST OF HEKATE

"All nature, resplendent in thy great glory, is raised up and summoned in thee to the very heights of splendour. Triumphant Queen, look on us in our exile so that, following in thy footsteps, we too may come to the blessed country of heaven."[102]

Harvest-time is brought on by the heavy, intense heat of the dying days of summer. Wheat is reaped and ground down to flour, with which Faithful bake bread in memory of the death and assumption into heaven of the Mother of the King. The Goddess, Virgin and Mother, shows Herself to be the Great Initiatrix. The Pale Leukothea of Candlemas becomes the Holy Shulamite of Wisdom, in whom the light-bearing avatar king encounters Fate. The Marys as an icon of Sophia, torch-carriers and ointment bearers, are echoed.

Prior to the Assumption, the Faithful call to mind the Transfiguration of Jesus, that moment in which his divinity is revealed to his close companions, before he begins his final journey toward Jerusalem.

Not long after the celebration of the Assumption comes the feast of the Beheading of St John the Baptist; a decapitation ordered by Herod, at the behest of Herodias and Salome.

"Cain's sickle reaches out once again…"[103]

102 (from) O Prima Virgo – Lefebvre, G 1959 *Saint Andrew Daily Missal* pp.1402 Liturgical Apostolate, Abbey of St Andrew Belgium   103. See Robin-the-Dart's *Cain: an agricultural myth?* republished in Oates, S 2012 *The Star Crossed Serpent Volume II* pp. 129 – 133 Mandrake of Oxford UK

Shulamite[104]

104. Gustave Moreau - *Song of Songs* 1893. Public Domain, Wiki Commons License.

MICHAELMAS

"But Michael bears Thy standard dread, And lifts the mighty cross on high. He in that sign the rebel powers Did with their dragon prince expel; And hurl'd them from the heaven's high towers, Down like a thunderbolt to hell." [105]

The Faithful, in the approach to the feast of St Michael the Archangel, prince of the heavenly host who flung Lucifer from the heights, and watched him fall into a blackberry bush, observe the feasts of the Birthday of the Virgin Mary, the Exaltation of the Holy Cross, and Our Lady of Sorrows. Here, the Faithful see the Mother of the king accompany Her Son to Calvary, and stand beside him as he undergoes his passion and death, and then to receive his body.

"Only half of Cain remains visible above the eliptic..." [106]

In Lucifer's fall from heaven to earth, at the hands of St Michael, the Faithful perceive yet more facets of themes of sacrifice within sacred marriage; the descent of Dumuzi, who is followed into the realms of the Dead by Holy Inanna; the ultimate sacrifice of the divine avatar who incarnates within the cycles of Time and Death, and another perspective on the origin and purpose of divine kingship. Michaelmas is followed by the feast of the Guardian Angels, offering, in that tide, a focus upon the Watchers; the 'Fallen Angels' who taught the civilising arts when the world was young.

The Hero[107]

105. (from) Te Splendor et Virtus - Lefebvre, G 1959 *Saint Andrew Daily Missal* Pp 1482 Liturgical Apostolate, Abbey of St Andrew Belgium   106. See Robin-the-Dart's *Cain: an agricultural myth?* republished in Oates, S 2012 *The Star Crossed Serpent Volume II* Pp. 129 - 133 Mandrake of Oxford UK 107. *St George* by Gustave Moreau 1889/90. Public Domain, Wiki Commons License.

ALL HALLOWS

"With Thy favoured sheep, O place me, Nor among the goats abase me, But to Thy right hand upraise me. While the wicked are confounded, Doomed to flames of woe unbounded, Call me with Thy saints surrounded."[108]

The earthly light and life of the avatar King now extinguished, he is entombed and journeys to the Place of his Ancestors. Having passed beyond the veil and across the River, his spirit, liberated from matter, is gathered up home again, and is free among the Dead. In the company

The Norns[109]

108. (from) Dies Iræ – Lefebvre, G 1959 *Saint Andrew Daily Missal* Pp 1584 Liturgical Apostolate, Abbey of St Andrew Belgium   109.Norns_(1832)_from_Die_Helden_ und_Götter_des_Nordens, Public Domain

of his Ancestors, he comes face to face with the bare bones of who he is

In the dark cave of the Norns, where is fed the roots of the world tree, he encounters She who spins, She who weaves, and She who cuts. The King, and those who have followed him into the tomb, come face to face with the core of their being.

The Faithful perceive that the virile King of Roodmas, having traced the path of his forebears, is also the dark Lord of the Mound who witnesses and ratifies ancient Covenants of Kinship and Clanship. In celebrations of All Hallows Eve, All Saints Day, and All Souls Day, in various popular pieties that characterise the month of the Holy Souls, and in the feasts of St Martin of Tours and the Presentation of the Blessed Virgin in the Temple, the Faithful renew ancestral covenants that reach beyond Time and Death, and re-commit themselves to following the Way of their Ancestors through this life and the next, to arrive at Her blessed halls.

"Cain almost sunk on the ecliptic, only his head can be seen."[110]

This is not the end, however, as the Knots flow from one into the next, and so the Faithful wait, in the quiet darkness of winter, to be resurrected with the light-bearing avatar at Christmas. The chaotic feasting that follows Midwinter is once again brought to a close at Twelfth Night, and the

---

110. See Robin-the-Dart's *Cain: an agricultural myth?* republished in Oates, S 2012 *The Star Crossed Serpent Volume II* pp. 129 - 133 Mandrake of Oxford UK

Faithful call to mind how the avatar rides out on a white horse, his eyes aflame, his head crowned, his robe dipped in blood, and a sword coming from his mouth, to gather up his People as the world perishes in fire and in water...

"[The Faith] can and does embrace the totality of human experience from birth to death, then beyond. It creates within the human spirit a light that brightens all darkness, and which can never again be extinguished."[111]

111. Cochrane, R 1965 *The Faith of the Wise* http://www.clanoftubalcain.org.uk/the_letters/FOTW_article_lk.pdf

THE
WORD MADE FLESH

Oral tradition has long been a part of our social communities; our languages link us back to our predecessors and we commune with them through our stories, myths, and songs. Additionally, oral transmission serves as a way of defining a collective identity and the continuity of a shared heritage. Language assumes mythological origins wherein the Word itself holds the creative impetus of thought and form.[112]

This sacred utterance fashions worlds as easily as it fashions our worldviews; as hearing, seeing, and speaking were not so clearly defined in relationship to Truth. Where the power of the Word commits to Truth, we may find Virtue. Where it fails to do so, we are left[113] only with the Lie. To know them both, is to know God. Our Word is our bond. Robert Cochrane, late Magister of the Clan of Tubal Cain, once stated that;

> *"The past moves in the future, since past shapes the future to come this is Fate. All things that are of this world belong to the past..., therefore the past lives on."* [113]

112. Shani Oates, *Make It So* http://clanoftubalcain.org.uk/makeso.html 113. Ibid

Highlighting the Providence of Fate, he asserts the burden of Time as the eternal Now in Wyrð; from this all things are created and recreated. Immersion within these mysteries engenders gnosis through engagement, in this all men are equal and are thus held as active participants in creation's dawn for:

"In Fate, and the overcoming of Fate, lies the true Graal."[114]

ODROERIR

From Muses to Giants, the art of poetry continues to be regarded as a gift of divine origin. Numerous myths retell the genesis of this noble craft as one of Her potencies. As an act of poiesis, the inspired Word is the emergent creative theophany of divine numina, an ekstasis outside of Space and Time where an Unio Mystica is achieved.

Inspiration; when mediated by Truth, Love, and Beauty, generates the evolution of spirit through this Grace.

INSPIRATION: (N.) ORIGIN

Middle English – enspire, from Old French inspirer, from Latin inspirare – 'breathe or blow into' from in 'into' + spirare 'breathe'.

The word was originally used of a divine or supernatural being, in the sense 'impart a truth or idea to someone.' Gold, Wealth, and Treasure are common themes within the Eddic poetry of the Northern traditions, often in relation to Female or Ancestral spirits. As guardians, they keep and

---

114 Robert Cochrane, Letter to Joe Wilson, http://clanoftubalcain.org.uk/the_letters/letters_Joe_Wilson_lk.pdf

Angel of Revelation[115]

115. *Angel of the Revelation* by William Blake, Public Domain, Wiki Commons License.

defend the forces of these treasures until a worthy heir is found. As Initiators, they reveal these treasures for what they truly are by trial and sacrifice. Often overlooked, their titanic prowess is woven throughout myth to approximate what must be intrinsically experienced. Within the poem Skáldskaparmál, we learn the source of the skaldic skill as being the dregs of the Poetic Mead, Óðrerir. This treasured elixir (and/or cauldron) so named Stirrer of Oðr or Inspiration, was attended by the giantess Gunnloð as its appointed custodian within her mountain dwelling.

By her leave, Óðinn stayed for three nights and drank three times from Óðrerir; from this came poetry to Man and to the Aesir. Places such as caves, gardens, and mountains reflect the corpus of sacred spaces so upheld in communities and clans as points of congress with the divine. [116] Medieval tradition held Mary as the 'hortus conclusus' or enclosed garden symbolizing paradise renewed through her as co-creatrix and mediatrix; the Song of Solomon echoes this often amatory association by stating:

"A garden enclosed is my sister, my spouse."

Burial mounds and chambers later gave way to ossuary's as locations of internment for the beloved dead, but discoveries have shown that caves were largely used in a similar atavistic way. Mountains, like caves, were inextricably linked to cultural identity through ancestral bonds as the womb/tomb.[117]

116. Shani Oates, The People of Goda, (Self published, 2012) pp56 – 57. 117. Tom D. Dillehay, Mounds of Social Death: Araucanian Funerary Rites and Political Succession, (1995)

Volva[118]

Many Eastern traditions recognize a sacred mountain as the navel of the world, the site where creation took place; a holy omphalos. These areas of worship became places of pilgrimage, often connected to specific tutelary deities; this is especially true for regions along the Indus Valley and the Himalayas, both areas of large migrations and trade.

By contemplating the story of Gunnlöð and the Poetic Mead much is to be noted, we will remember that as a giantess she is primordial, before the gods; springing from Ymir her form is as an ancestral presiding genius. These 'mothers' are noted within the sagas as Jotun brides, listed as Gerðr, Hlodyn, Eir and Menglöð among others, all expressing implications of protection and stewardship beneath Her mantle.[119]

118. Skáldskaparmál Saga – Project Gutenberg. 119. Gerðr, Hloydn, Eir, and Menglöð: Listed as nine (sometimes thirteen) in total. Gerðr (Enclosed), Hloydn (Protector of the Hearth), Eir is of unknown etymology but possibly associated with healing, and Menglöð (The one who takes pleasure in jewels).

Where mythology has presented this reckoning through erotic allegory (entering of her mound) we can deduce alternatively, that it is a shift to a higher reasoning of Henosis, the Marriagebed betwixt Force and Form. Her light, her gifts, are meted by him through Sacrifice and Duty; the passage "three nights and three draughts" is indicative of an initiatory experience, one night for every sip.

The name Gunnloð[120] reflects this quite beautifully as Battle/Gift of Love; however this battle is one of ego, only through its submission can we receive Her Love. Chthonic associations of Her mountain/mound home makes further reference to ancestral streams; but again also to Life, to Love, and to Fate. As Lover, she lures us forth, as Mother, and thereby Death, She 'gathers us back home again.' Within her embrace is the source of All.

Her Mead then, is to be understood as the reward of Spirit through Gyfu; the highest principle of reciprocity in troth between kin.

By entering Her mountain, we meet 'death' in the sacrifice of self, but all is renewed within her cauldron, that we may know Wisdom; the Castle Perilous.

This premise is what Cochrane's 'Witch Law' confirms, urging us to 'take all we are given, and give all of ourselves.' For Óðrerir and Oðr are both indicative of inspiration, but also of inheritance; and it is Oðal which holds that place of tradition, estate, and familial kin(g)ship within the runic futhark to be Oð's men! As for gold, wealth, and treasure;

120. Raimo Anttila, Greek and Indo-European Etymology in Action: Proto Indo European, (John Benjamins BV, 2000) 86

Parsifal revealing the Holy Grail[121]

Her mead is above all worldly possessions.

It is (The People of) Goda.

121. Detail from *Parcival shows the Holy Grail*, detail from an illustration, circa 1894 by Theodor Pixis. Public Domain, Wiki Commons License.

"The well-earned beauty | well I enjoyed, Little the wise man lacks; So Othrörir now | has up been brought to the midst of the men of earth."

THE HÁVAMÁL – CENNANMAN

CENNAN: (V.) ORIGIN: Old English: make known, declare, acknowledge.

The CennanMan is one who upholds the meaning of Word and Deed, as his Word 'bonds' him to the People through her gift of inspiration. This singular belief permeates through all we are and all we do in Truth; to abide in honour with our gods, our kin, and with ourselves.

Holy Grail[122]

122. *The Damsel of the Sanct Grael*, by Dante Gabriel Rossetti 1874. Public Domain, Wiki Commons License.

We come to drink from her cup, to 'know' and by 'knowing,' become the craftsman of our own destinies. She affords us this choice in faith and trust, not to win a good life, but to win a good Fate. As knowledge rests between thought and action, we can say with all certainty that this is the Craft of the Wise.

"I am the loved and beloved

I am the lover and his mate

I am the well without water,

From which I am the whole and the part

I am compassion healing pain

I am diamond cutting stone hearts.

I am a mirror without reflection.

All must drink.

I am words, love and words

Yea! but never speak."[123]

123. Excerpt from *The Ash Tree* by Roy Bowers

STRENGTH IN YOUR ARMS

'Most gracious Lady, when I fall,
Hold me.

When filled with Love, but am greeted with Hate,
Comfort me.

When I give all, And my body breaks,
Heal me.

If words fail, And deeds falter,
Teach me.

In times of solitude, lost in creation,
Know me

If this death, Be all for naught,
Mourn me.

When gathered Home, And at your side,
Love me.[124]

---

124 Ulric "Gestumblindi" Goding – Initially published online under the pseudonym "Cunning Apostle" in 2012.

SACRED DANCE
& SACRED FIRE

Trance and magical dancing finds its origins in the Palaeolithic, where tribal peoples would achieve emotional and rhythmic unity between themselves and their totem animal and/or tutelary deity, which sometimes, but not always, were one-and-the same thing. In these proto- shamanic communities, dancers adopted the guise of certain animals by wearing horns, skin and tail; and usually by the one chosen to lead the dance. It was believed that an altered state facilitated communication with spirits of animals hunted for food, and of the greatly revered ancestral hunters of the tribe to whom they appealed for aid.

Dance was also a significant feature of Dionysian religion, whose ecstatic practices released its aspirants from their individuality to merge with God consciousness. To be fully effective, the ego needs to be shaken off and cast aside. This requires trust and practice. Releasing our grip upon the ego is no easy task, but in time, the measure of discipline will lead to greater lucidity within ritual, a greater intensity and the increased awareness/sensitivity to subliminal experiences.

Both exhaustion and pain/suffering also lead to transcendence, but without 'will,' consequential pain can often become the 'end' to the 'means', degenerating into an exercise in sado-masochism. Pain (generally induced by feats of endurance and/or scourging), should only be exercised in order to shatter the limits of human consciousness/awareness – to open the door, to cross the threshold of conceptual, cognitive responses. Pain is merely a tool; it should only ever be the 'means' to a pre-determined and focussed 'end'. However, over-indulgence or exceeding the brief is almost always counter-productive, rendering the whole exercise pointless, often voiding the entire magical enterprise.

Exhaustion, through dancing, fasting, physical strains,

Shamanic Dancing to the Moon[125]

125. *Grete Wiesenthal's Ecstatic Danube Waltzes*, 1908, photographed by Arnold Genthe. Public Domain, Wiki Commons License.

sex and laughter, can, in most cases be the simplest and most effective techniques of achieving altered states. Everyone has different limits and tolerances; push yourself, aspire to exceed them, but slowly and safely.

A reed may bend with gentle and persistent manipulation but will snap if pressed too firmly. Exhaustion dissolves conscious identity, creating a vacuum, a state of in-between-ness into which revelations seep. Pain and crises are mere thresholds of endurance, part of a cyclical pattern of evolution.....to move away from something, one must move towards it. But how much crisis and dissolution is needed? For extreme pain does not induce extreme enlightenment! Ego determines the level of intensity required to break down the formality of identity and control.......first exhaustion, then void of ego consciousness, then channelling through oneself.

Remember also, that living fully at the edge of your reality living every moment in your magic, in prayer and in full awareness of your magical argosy will facilitate a far quicker transition into altered states, than those aspirants whose compartmentalised lifestyle causes frustrating delays. Like an underground stream, awareness should trickle away beneath the surface, ready to swell and erupt when needed, vitalised by every heartbeat. This is true will. Your life should be a living talisman for your magic, an articulation/ expression of perceived cumulative experience, manifest in every moment.

Traditionally, Roodmas, May's Eve or Beltane – the feast of good fires, heralds the time for merrymaking, for welcoming in the Summer, for joy at the renewed vigour in plant, man and beast. This single rite more than many, is suited to the 'dance', erotic, ecstatic, shamanic or simply celebratory. But upon looking closer, we may discern that such activities 'mask' an even deeper celebration, for these

Foliate Head[126]

126. Carvings from the pew ends on the Church of the Holy Ghost, Crowcombe, Somerset. Dating from 1535. Photo credit to Jacqui Ross from Somerset, England. 2013 Public Domain, Wiki Commons License

things remain within the bounds of the outer mysteries, the exoteric; they are 'apart' from the true core significance of this time in the ritual year.

The old Oak King is on the Wane...this is the time of the Holly King, the sensual, erotic reveller, the shaman initiator, the 'Lord of the Dance' – the Solar King who reveals the true meaning of 'Beltane', the fire quickening in the blood, in life, fecund and verdant. Just as in an exoteric, mundane sense, Beltane signifies the release of cattle from barns and pens, from their winter confinement, so it is that esoterically we are also released from our confines of the introspections of Winter. The doorway offers us an escape, a release into another world where we are once more free to explore and expand our occult faculties.

Roodmas, May's Eve or Beltane celebrates this freedom of mental expansion, of growth induced by the awakening of the spirit within. Moreover, the avatar of initiation – Al Khidir, the spirit of the Green Man, triggers all this activity. Outwardly, he represents the fecundity of nature, of new life, re-generation and its fertility rites, themes that 'mask' his true virtues. Green tendrils issue from silent lips, breathing life and energy into oracular powers and divine speech, wisdom rises from his roots, rising like sap in to fresh growth, sprouting from these masked sprits, 'guised' aspects of primal energy. Throughout many ancient cultures, ranging from Slavonic peoples to Indo-Aryans, from Europeans to Egyptians, the colour green represents secret initiatory aspects, especially prevalent when combined with Horns and animal skins.

Later 'Celtic' language peoples absorbed these understandings into their histories and mythologies, transmuting the colour green into that of 'Fey', the hidden people, our ancestors, guides and muses. Within Sufi tradition, the Green Prophet, (Al Khidir), drinks the waters of immortality and spends eternity initiating all seekers. May' Eve balances Hallows' Eve in the ritual year as diurnal portals into the 'Other' worlds paralleled in liminal time, places of great age, secrets, of death, truth knowledge and wisdom. Polarised aspects of life and death, represented by the symbols of each seasonal avatar, peer out through the foliate mask of the Green Man, and the Skull and Crossbones

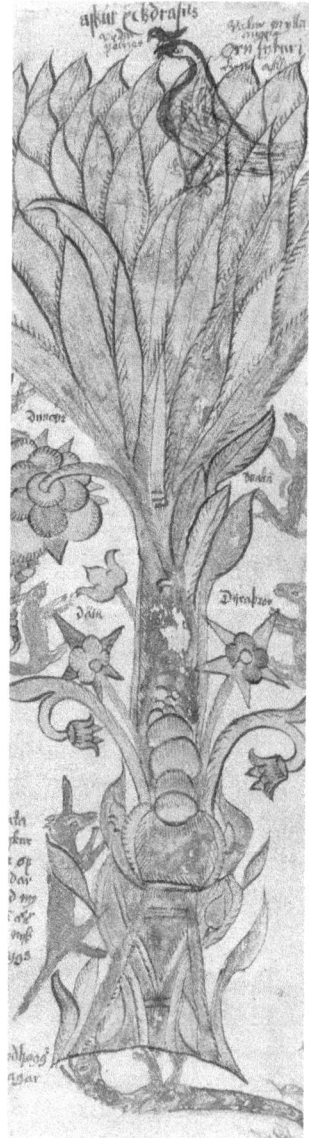

Yggdrasil[127]

127. Public Domain

of the Reaper. The Man in Green (Robin) becomes the Man in Black (Harlequin).

Nine magical woods (oak, ash, hazel, alder, elder, willow, birch, rowan and hawthorn make up the balefire), each one an offering to their associative dedicated deities, are invoked for protection and illumination during the journey. The Maypole too possesses deeper significance as the cosmic axis; when placed within the Omphalos (the epicentre of our creation) it facilitates release upwards into the other worlds, the outer realm of astral levels and altered realities. Effectually, it becomes the shamanic pole (Axis Mundi) utilised by our European ancestors for thousands of years, which also takes us down into the underworld at All Hallows' Eve.

Indeed, it still serves this function for indigenous peoples such as the Yakut Shamans in the East and for the long-suffering Aboriginal tribes that populate Australia.

Attached by ribbons (representing vines), all celebrants circumambulate, winding round and round the cosmic pole, the nexus of the sacred tree that binds the power of the Sun, Moon and Stars down to Earth, acting as a conduit, entwining all within the cosmic dance of time and space. This cosmic 'Mill' is thus frenzied, being more evocative of the ecstatic rite of Dionysus (also a horned 'green' deity associated with initiatory and experiential rites), whose revellers also wore masks of vines and laurel (hallucinogenic), both evergreen....... eternal as the soul on its eternal cyclic journey towards enlightenment.

Dance of Creation

Shiva, A 10th century Chola dynasty bronze sculpture of Nataraja. Public Domain, Wiki Commons License.

Interestingly, the orgiastic rites of Sabarar (Shiva) in India directly parallel these masked rites of ancient Thrace, Asia Minor and Crete. He becomes the medium for prophecy as man and plant spirit align in purpose, the 'Holy Fool', the wild and wise 'Woodwose', the serpent, disgorging and devouring itself within its own universe to become the living tree of knowledge. This 'Summer Lord' brings harmony through disruption, synthesis through symbiosis and renewal through regeneration. As 'Nataraja' he dances creation into form, inspiring poets, seers, dancers to follow in his wake.

And so, our leaping here is no simple act of sympathetic magic to induce the crops to grow, but serves to stimulate the rush of endorphins in to bloodstream to enhance our transition into altered states – a shamanic shift into true Sabbatic flight.

The 'Leader of the Dance', resplendent in foliate mask and phallic club (reflecting his role as initiator), instigates a quickening, leading his followers into the circle where everyone dances until exhausted.

Thereafter to explore their own journeys in a meditative state of light trance; thus the Wild Man is invoked upon this Sabbat, through dancing and journeying as the guide to our re-awakening. But the Creatrix, the Shakti force to His form, is not forgotten in these rites for through Her expression of creative sovereignty, balance is achieved, harmonising the fiery impetuosity of God energy. She confers the right to be yourself, to discover your True Will and to explore its boundaries magically – a gift for true expansion.

A MIDSUMMER NIGHT'S DREAM: DREAMING THE DARK!

"I know a bank whereon the wild thyme blows,
Where cowslips and the nodding violet grows.
Quite over-canopied with lush woodbine,
Where sweet musk-roses with eglantine;
There sleeps Titania sometime of the night,
Lull'd in these flowers with dances and delight"[128]

Throughout the history of ecstatic dance, it is not uncommon for participants to imbibe nature's own entheogens. Indeed, such enhancements are deemed as an almost obligatory accompaniment to sacred rituals. These traditions have to a greater and lesser extent become embedded within the Traditional Craft, most particularly in the attendant fields of 'witchcraft.' Across the ages, many plants have been ascribed special significance due to their propensity to induce spectacular, visionary and prophetic dreams.

Particular plants have proved popular, cropping up in diverse locations and throughout many centuries with little fluctuation. Throughout the Old World, Mesoamerica, and Southern Continents, narcotic beverages have been administered to the 'seers' of a given tribe, culled from herbs sacred to them specifically, to ensure favourable results.

128. William Shakespeare: *A Midsummer Night's Dream*

Thiselton-Dyer[129] explores particular examples of visionary narcotics used extensively by Amazon tribes peoples and by the Californian Indians, quite beautifully and concisely in his little book. And although his study is focussed upon the New World, the natural inclinations of tribal activities indicate little variance throughout the Old World also. Children, quite sensitively subject to hallucinatory effects, were guided through prophetic visions to garner specific information about their enemies. Similarly, Thiselton-Dyer proceeds to note how

Mandrake[130]

the Darien Indians used the seeds of the Datura sanguinca to exploit their delirium. Subsequent research reveals how this allowed tribal elders to resolve problems and assist them towards the acquisition of needful resources. Medicine-men of the Delaware drank intoxicating decoctions to incur extraordinary vision-quests.

Tobacco too was highly honoured by many of the North American tribes as a plant for stimulating a 'supernatural ecstasy.' In North Carolina, a common practice involved

129. Chapter IX – The Folk-Lore Of Plants by T.F. Thiselton-Dyer 1889.
130. *Mandragora Mann und Frau* 1491. In, *Hortus sanitates.* Unknown author. Public Domain, Wiki Commons License.

the removal of moss taken from the grave of a murder victim that is worn sported as an amorous amulet to beguile the attraction of a would-be lover. Held and inhaled while dreaming, it returns an errant stray lover home again.

The medieval 'Doctrine of Signatures' expressed the essential 'oneness' of being, and was drafted into magic, medicine and astrology by physicians and researchers of all 'Natural magics.' Numerous superstitions pertaining to the dream-inducing effects of plants have survived within several common sources of modern European folk-lore. We hear of how a much treasured four-leaved clover, a mystical symbol also associated with prosperity, is placed under a pillow by a would be lover to dream of his lady-love; daisy-roots and the rustic maiden serve a similar function.

Further east, the 'son-trava' dream herb, now identified as 'Pulsatilla patens,' blooms in April with the most stunning azure-coloured flower, and once placed under a pillow, all dreams thereafter are claimed to be fulfilled. Taking a shift from the ground to the heavenly canopy, the Elm tree, known as the 'tree of dreams' was used by Virgil in his epic tale – Aeneid, to forecast the oracle, an object of powerful prophecy.

Other flowers indicate prosperity in life; among which the violet and the vine dominate history. The pregnant mother of Cyrus the Great was recorded as having dreamed of a glorious lush and prolific vine.

Plants foretelling good fortune when seen in dreaming include the palm-tree, olive, jasmine, lily, laurel, thistle, thorn, wormwood, currant, pear, with the most fortuitous being the rose (though not white). Longevity and prosperity are naturally supplied by the advantageous reverie of such obvious candidates as the oak, apricot, apple, box, grape, and fig.

Yarrow or woundwort, named for Achilles (achillia millifolium) a hero instructed by Chiron in the arts of herb-lore, is a much prized and versatile fragile looking herb with many interesting properties. Held over the eyes, it is said to bestow the 'sight,' yet is also advisedly strewn across the bedcovers on Midsummer's Eve to avert the antics of the spiteful fey. It has acquired another more sinister use according to folk-lore, where love-sick maidens are instructed to seek out a young man's grave, upon which this mystical plant grows freely.

Plucking the freshest leaves they must recite the following charm, which typically incorporates Christian elements into the simple folk-magic of the period:

"Yarrow, sweet yarrow, the first that I have found, In the name of Jesus Christ I pluck it from the ground; As Jesus loved sweet Mary and took her for His dear, So in a dream this night I hope my true love will appear." [131]

In truth, many plants fulfil the role of 'love-divination,' though none so popular as the rose. Within dream flora further popular plants that auger well for affairs of the heart are the raspberry, pomegranate, cucumber, currant, and box.

---

131. Ibid. It is worthy of note here, regarding this particular charm that its publication precedes the discovery of both the Nag Hamaddi Gnostic gospels and the Dead Sea Scrolls that allude to this only recently acknowledged special relationship between Mary and Jesus.

Mary Magdalena[132]

Certain flowers though, remain fixed within the calendar itself, relating to particular seasonal customs. Various festivals generate a prolific interest and activity. For example, Midsummer's Eve, is extremely popular for numerous flower charms. Another delightful example requires nine different kinds of bloom (preferably in a chaplet) again placed beneath the pillow or head of he/she to dream of their sweetheart to come.

Mugwort and plantain have long associations with Midsummer, when young maids would search anxiously beneath the plants among their roots for a particular growth, a 'coal' (dark or wizened root) that when plucked on this eve only, would be placed beneath their pillows,

132. Bernadino Campi, *Mary 'Magdalena'* Google Art Project. unknown artist between 1522 and 1590. Public Domain, Wiki Commons License

Green Magic[133]

133. Dioscorides_Par_Gr_2179_f_11r_*Chamaileon*, 9th C. Public Domain, Wiki Commons License.

securing prophetic dreams of husbands to be. Sage leaves, twelve in total, mindfully plucked, held up to one's face and crushed at midnight on Midwinter's Eve conjures the shade of one's husband to be. Holly is another favourite used by lovers in various charms, particularly again at Midwinter and Midsummer, less so at All Hallows and Day of Janus. Here is a recipe and method for a typical folk-charm endorsed by many a young maid:

"Before retiring to rest, place three pails full of water in her bedroom, and then pin to her night-dress three leaves of green holly opposite to her heart, after which she goes to sleep. Believing in the efficacy of the charm, she persuades herself that she will be roused from her first slumber by three yells, as if from the throats of three bears, succeeded by as many hoarse laughs. When these have died away, the form of her future husband will appear, who will show his attachment to her by changing the position of the water-pails, whereas if he have no particular affection he will disappear without even touching them."[134]

St John's wort, the summer herb, sacred also to Baldr is a potent herb for use in divination, though it must be gathered on Midsummer's Eve. This is the trick, as it is said to carry off the picker on a fairy horse for a wild ride, only to be dropped hours later, miles from home. Sprigs of the evergreen Myrtle, sacred again to Aphrodite were kept under a bride's pillow to ensure the constancy of her lover. Mattresses stuffed with the soft and fragrant new

134. Chapter IX. *The Folklore of Plants* by T.F. Thiselton-Dyer 1889.

beech leaves whisper gently to all lovers asleep upon them, pervading their dreams with imaginative and complex tales and stories.

St. Valentine's Day is observed with various charms for would be lovers; one requires the pinning of bay leaves to each corner and centre of the sleeper's pillow, again with the intention of inducing the image of one's future husband. Another dream-inducing variation of this charm involves the simple preparation of two freshly plucked bay leaves, which must be sprinkled liberally with rosewater. The soaked leaves are then placed upon the pillow beside the would-be dreamer who will benefit from their aromas as they recite the following single phrase, over and over until they fall asleep.".

"Good Valentine, be kind to me, In dream let me my true love see."

Another, more involved process almost guaranteed to produce successful results was performed on St. Luke's Day, where the dreamer is instructed to:

"Take marigold flowers, a sprig of marjoram, thyme, and a little wormwood; dry them before a fire, rub them to powder, then sift it through a fine piece of lawn; simmer these with a small quantity of virgin honey, in white vinegar, over a slow fire; with this anoint your stomach, breasts, and lips, lying down, and repeat these words thrice:–

'St Luke, St. Luke, be kind to me, In dream let me my true love see!'

This said, hasten to sleep, and in the soft slumbers of night's repose, the very man whom you shall marry shall appear before you." [135]

135 .Ibid

Dew collected from the Lady's Mantle was allegedly used to seek and procure the famed philosophers stone, yet its crushed petals assisted in peaceful dreamless sleep. This is contra to the fragrant honeysuckle and hops that induce erotic dreams featuring in many a lover's summer bower. However, dreaming of fruit or flowers out of season is perceived as ill-omens of woe:

"A bloom upon the apple-tree when the apples are ripe, Is a sure termination to somebody's life."

And once more, according to an old Sussex adage:

"Fruit out of season, Sounds out of reason."[136]

Mythical vines offer a sacred connection to the 'other' providing a medium of communication between the world of the living and the dead. But more intriguing is the fact that this 'contact' actually appears to the 'spirit-worker as a two-way ladder by which the 'Ojibways' traverse between earth and the opposing end they believe to be twined round a Star. Images drawn from this travelling are retained as pictograms, glyphs collected over time as the memory of the dreaming prophecies for these people. They provide a visual record of the power they wield as gifted workers in that field.

Anthropologists, having studied such examples alongside other folk records are able to conclude that dreaming of white flowers invariably forecasts a death. Comparable to this is the superstition surrounding the sudden outburst of the blooms of the alba rose, taken as a sure sign of the imminent death to the dweller closest to it.

In Scottish ballads the birch is 'feminine' presence again is long associated with the dead:

"I dreamed a dreary dream last nicht;
God keep us a' frae sorrow!
I dreamed I pu'd the birk sae green,
Wi' my true love on Yarrow.
I'll redde your dream, my sister dear,
I'll tell you a' your sorrow;
You pu'd the birk wi' your true love;
He's killed, – he's killed on Yarrow."[137]

Dreaming of the yew tree foretells the death of an older person whose wealth will provide a substantial legacy. Dreaming while subject to the soporific fumes of the yew tree signifies the alteration of the brain's chemistry, resulting in chaotic imagery related to sex and death. This hypnotic perfume is a potent aphrodisiac, similar to the mandrake. Intriguingly, both the yew and the mandrake are linked to chthonic deities, holding the virtues of love, death and sleep/dreams (Aphrodite, Hypnos and Thanatos), drawing them together as the 'triple bane' under the auspices of the single and enchanting patroness of these not so subtle potencies. The fragrant and delicate meadowsweet or 'queen of the meadows' is another heavy soporific from whose influence the dreamer may never awaken.

136. Margaret Baker: *The Folklore of Plants*, Shire publications ltd 1996 p.76
137. Ibid

The fateful 'atropa belladonna' or beautiful fair [pale?] lady gifts the 'sight', but also madness and death. Used externally as bewitchments, it may be worn as a chaplet across the temples and crown. Plants that are seen as those of ill omen denote misfortune: plum, cherry, withered roses, walnut, hemp, cypress, dandelion and garlic.

Herb Robert, an invasive wild flower is cautioned against picking, as its nickname 'death come quickly' reveals; or 'if

Atropa Belladonna.
Publish'd as the Act directs by D.' Woodville Jan.71. 1790.

Belladonna[138]

138. *Atropa Belladonna – Medical Botany 1790-01* Public Domain, Wiki Commons License.

ee pick'n someone'll take ee.'

Beans, oddest of all, again associated with the Pale Leukothea, incur great terrors and grief in plenty-fold! Sleeping in a bean field is said to induce horrific nightmares and sometimes even death! Folk-lore gifts to them the anchor of the departed soul, haunting the earth, spiralling upwards, seeking new life. Thyme is another herb believed to attract and 'hold' the souls of the dead, through the punning of its name 'time', a quality given only to the living. It is therefore never included in funereal wreaths. On the other hand, rosemary sprigs under the bed avert the haunting of spirits and nightmare imagery, the pungent aroma keeping all ill at bay.

Held by many as the definitive sacred symbol of the Universal Goddess, the bramble vine of white flowers and black/red fruits plays a considerable divinatory role, as we should expect from this tenacious and glorious plant.

"To dream of passing through places covered with brambles portends troubles; if they prick you, secret enemies will do you an injury with your friends; if they draw blood, expect heavy losses in trade." To dream of being pricked with briars, shows that the person dreaming has an ardent desire to something, and that young folks dreaming thus are in love, who prick themselves in striving to gather their rose." [139]

And there ends and begins another tale, of distaff, needle, ladies fair and foul, all spirit wanderers in weal and woe.

139. Op.Cit. Baker 1996

Шиповничек

Briar Rose[140]

140. Arthur Rackham, *Sleeping Beauty*, Public Domain, Wiki Commons License.

OF SKALDS, SCOPS & PUNS

"A scop was a poet as represented in Old English poetry.
The scop is the Anglo-Saxon counterpart of the Old
Norse skald, with the important difference that "skald"
was applied to historical persons while "scop" is used, for
the most part, to designate oral poets within Old English
literature. There is very little information known about the
mythical scop and its existence is still under debate."[141]

We should remember that in time, the Scop became scoff and Skald became scold. However, the above quote appears to address the dilemma of doubt regarding the intent and rationale behind Bowers' passionate assertion of the 'Faith' through his beliefs and practises. His work is a curious blend of religion and philosophy, by which principles his views present a seeming paradox.

"It is characteristic of the Germanic tradition of poetry that the
sacred or heroic cannot be separated from the ecstatic or drunken state,
and correspondingly crude jesting (compare the Lokasenna, where
the poet humorously depicts the gods themselves as quarrelsome and
malicious), qualities summed up in the concept of *woþuz, the name-
giving attribute of the god of poetry, *Wodanaz."

141. *A History of Oral Interpretation* by Eugene and Margaret Bahn. 1970. Minneapolis: Burgess Publishing.

Flyting – Scoffing[142]

In order to tackle this philosophical conundrum, we must first consider the restrictions imposed by Plato especially. He is at the root of the mainstream of Western Philosophy and many contradictory tendencies derive from him. The most valuable thing handed down to us by Plato is the thread of critical thought, something so utterly different to either belief or opinion, it allows opinion to bond with its opposite, becoming argument and thus, possibly, expose the truth.

Much of what we deem to be a paradox is more often, a lack of comprehension; ignorance removes us from the

142. Lokasenna (1895) by Lorenz Frølich. Public Domain, Wiki Commons License.

power of rational argument and objective conclusion. Discernment follows our understanding, and understanding is the work itself.

Therefore, we may only shift our view and modify opinion in line with our grasp of the Mysteries. It is therefore less that Bowers speaks through paradox in true riddles per se, but instead, utilised the only means he has available to discuss and explain the Mysteries. This he adequately explains to Joe Wilson when he tells him that the People teach by using poetic inference. We cannot define the infinite; we can merely point to it.

The signs and symbols are all available to this end, just like a signpost may be written in many languages yet say a similar thing. On the one hand, getting beyond the language barrier and grasping the concept is to open a door of perception, whilst initially the paradox and riddle may perplex and baffle. It is a case of the finger pointing at the moon, again.

The paradox or riddle seems to be so, merely because we are unable to fathom a definition of interpretation according to the faculties accessed under the limit of experience available to draw from. His methods on the one hand was to use a Socratic teaching mechanism, and on the other, to 'test' confuse and throw glamour over those he wished to employ his 'grey' magic upon.

Even this may be interpreted as an attempt to trigger a shift in perception. There is a widely-held assumption that Bowers' claims and statements are false, believing him to be a deliberate trickster who conned and bamboozled

Reynard the Fox[143]

everyone. Those people might instead consider the possibility that Bowers was in fact, using illusion and delusion, to point to the truth.".

Bards and philosophers have long exploited the veil of illusion to reveal its deception; inferential concepts composed of poetic kennings and/or references are used

143. *Reynard the fox*, drawn by Ernest Henri Griset. 1869. Public Domain. (PD-ART.)

not in the old 'challenge' sense (competitively). However, most of what he presents to us *does* operate as a true riddle in that there is no actual definition to his punning. These apprehensions generate an oblique vocabulary, revealed through obfuscation. It is pure Zen in principle if not application:

"It is in seeking that one finds the answers."

Yet there is no end while so ever mind and body remain conjoined. Conundrums, puzzles, riddles, puns etc., provoke, prickle and permeate the peripatetic rational of lateral exploration, to which lapwings abound, the Roebuck presides over, and the dog bares his teeth at.

All is distraction. It is: *'not this, not that.'*

Roy Bowers references Taliesin, the arcane bard who used well the art of riddling. Such riddles force us to cogitate on visionary evocation and logistical kenning until we reach the conclusion in a flash of apprehension – realisation within the 'other.'

When working within the Mysteries, we must avoid where possible, all self-imposed restrictions that may stifle our understanding of cultural sources.

There is certainly a single all-pervading spirit that runs through the work and is the One Source, and yet the Muse freely emerges without restraint. So, refining our path to a single definition to the exclusion of even peripheral influences, is self-defeating in our desire to encounter fulfilment within the mysteries 'proper.'

Across Europe and throughout the Middle-East, there has been a seething community of substantial confluence. Germanic peoples and 'Vikings' enjoyed empires spanning much of the equatorial basin and into Byzantium and Asia.

The questions, riddles and mysterious glyphs may at different times offer a direct solution to a technical problem of ritual, a philosophical or mystical insight, or a deeply sceptical view on what is most uncertain, holding the mental doors wide open as it were, and sometimes seemingly all at once.

This extract from a piece written several years ago

Merlin & Nimue[144]

144. Doré - Vivien Pa II, Merlin and Nimue, Public Domain, Wiki Commons License.

was an initial attempt to explore how Bowers managed to synthesise both modalities within his work. Following on this, I suppose the obvious question would be, how and where do we even begin?

To aid in that amazing journey of self-discovery, these ciphers now transcribed according to the Mythos and teachings of the 'Clan of Tubal Cain' and transmitted 'mouth to ear' by the late Magister, Evan John Jones. He would often become wryly amused when asked about these symbols and other points covered within the Bowers' letters, he was prone to remark with a wink:

"I was there in the room when he typed most of them you know – we discussed much of it between us."

FOOL

A Mentor of mine, instructing me in the arts of symbolism, specifically within the Tarot, paused momentarily before delivering an explanation of one of the major arcana, which was not only unfamiliar to me, but quite challenging. I had drawn the Fool. At that time, I received the explanation as a slight.

An offence.

Struggling with comprehension, I could only imagine that I must appear – well 'foolish' in some way. In retrospect I now understand its inferences to a person who is gauche, naive - an innocent blundering upon their way, unaware of all they encounter, unable to 'see' what lies ahead, distracted by the 'now'. Not a folly, just blinkered with a lack, a void of 'something' less tangible. Hence the zero placement. – the empty slate… a seeker of pure heart and mind as yet unsullied by preconception or prejudice and as yet unshaped by experience and gnosis.

And so the 0 card, the one we know as 'The Fool' is a portrait of a pilgrim that is far from being simplistic.

Of all the characters in the Tarot Quest, it is the only one to exhibit movement, although it appears to poise on the spot, striding forwards, whilst looking backwards. Therefore, all movement is both implicit and explicit simultaneously.

The Fool is everywhere and nowhere, without the true guidance of purposeful orientation. And this is exactly what and where their path leads them to understand throughout their quest.

The Fool[145]

145. *Sola Busca* Tarot Deck, Public Domain, Wiki Commons License.

Often depicted carrying a pig's bladder, to signify they own nothing but the wit of honest humour, sans satire - their 'baggage, which at this point is light and hardly deemed a burden, is their only 'possession.' It is all they have acquired thus far on that journey. The observer may deduce from this the empty vessel in readiness for all that is yet to come their way.

A Tabula Rasa.

For nothing of consequence propels them or prepares them for what lies ahead. A Nomad you might suggest?

In a way, most certainly.

Perhaps it is an expression of the repeated incarnations of all journeymen, where all that was learned before is not to be immediately tapped into or available at will, but must be awakened slowly, by event and encounter with the other and with our earthly guides through whom they work and instruct all.

Their journey, the continuing quest is evident in the way this character is portrayed. Their untainted enthusiasm is pure and without guile. Maybe the Fool, having drunk from the waters of Oblivion river, has been around enough to know better after all?

Who then is the Fool?

A riddle that does not unravel.

Warp & Weft of Time[146]

146. *Old woman with distaff.* Anonymous (Italy) . Public Domain, Wiki Commons License.

In the name of the Mask

I believe it is a known fact that the use of masks in ritual is common amongst several of those traditions known as traditional witchcraft, otherwise known as families or clans.

But of what and how do we make them?

What does it represent and do?

What follows is my own personal experience on the subject. The making of the mask itself, is a profound spiritual exercise that leads one on a journey of un-forseen self-discovery. The mask takes the shape of one's totem animal or what is commonly known as the inner-beast. So here perhaps is where I should explain what that means to myself before I proceed further.

When I was trying to make contact with my own beast, I was unsure on how to even begin. So I made the usual mistake of analysing my traits faults and personality so find an affinity to a suitable species.

The result of course was an animal that in character was

similar to my mundane self. But that was far from the truth, that emerged later.…..The beast itself does, however, come forth once invoked, and once contact is made, all doubts dissolve.

The way it manifests its clues are very apparent. So much so that at first one tends to disregard them as fantasy. In my case it was as simple as seeing an image of it everywhere, from shopping bags to dreaming it.. Once I actually heard its call with my own ears and had it confirmed that I wasn't 'hearing things' by unbiased persons that knew not what I was about, I let it through.

Here is where the seeker finds oneself at a crossroads, and by their own free will a choice. Face the Truth or live a lie. I now know that such questioning presents and represents itself throughout our corporeal existence. For me the mask was the catalyst that set my awareness of Wyrð in motion. The mask itself embodies and conceals our true self. It is also the means for one of our hardest tasks, of the journey facing ego. What is ego?

The first definitions you will find in the dictionary will be as follows, or similar.

1. A person's sense of self-esteem or self-importance.

2. The part of the mind that mediates between the conscious and the unconscious and is responsible for reality testing and a sense of personal liberty.

3. In metaphysics, it is a conscious subject

Though, it is probably all three.

In the presence of deity, our ancestors, brothers and sisters, we unmask ourselves. In truth an honour and by our own free will, we reveal all.

This can and does take us out of our comfort zone, after all we lived thus covered for a long time. At this stage we take a name. Some will take other names according to their development.

A Sardonic Mask[147]

147. Sardonic Mask, Public Domain, Wiki Commons License.

Others will keep their given name from their ritual Initiations and/or Inductions and Admissions. I found that in most cases, in this day and age, members will continue to call each other by their everyday name.

Spiritual/magical names are used in most traditions as a sign of birth and re-birth but what does it mean? A hint can be found even in the monastic orders of the Catholic Church. We die to all ignorance and all that is outside the Sacred Hearth. We leap between the dimensions of the quick and the departed. We sail with the Ferryman but we're not dead! We sail the river of oblivion but do not drink from it. We've taken the physical mask off but we do not sever the link with humanity.

The Mask is a Bridge.

It is a facet of Lucifer, The Holy Ghost:

Communion, river-between, crossroads, scapegoat and everything that links us to the Source of all.

A life-well lived; a worthy sacrifice.

RE-FORGE AND TEMPER

Everything has a past, this is inescapable. One's past and the steps taken henceforth is that which forges the Wyrð of the Soul. Onwards and upwards is the direction sought, for stasis is non-existence. All isn't forgiven and the slate not wiped clean upon prostrating to a 'cosmic saviour'. Personal salvation is just that -personal. Re-forge and temper until one's character or soul is that of worth. Word and deed hold consequences that inherently shape further possible words and deeds or limitations thereof; consideration is a must, lest one falls foul of being ensnared in a woeful trap of their own making.

Life is a gift from the Old Ones, this 'middle-enclosure' existence of ours is here for the experience of the soul. It isn't something to be shunned, wished away in the hope of a glowing reality up in the clouds. We are to live life fully, live life honourably, to live life well.

No, we are not our brother's keeper but let us remember that when we are but dust scattered across the winds it will be our names and associated deeds that will be left behind; left as either a legacy to inspire or a folly to be quickly forgotten.

It has also been said that:

'no man is an island…..'[148]

Though be mindful of who is invited into the tapestry of your Wyrð, as once allowed, threads shall be entwined and Wyrð weaves further accordingly, threads cannot be undone and removed, tears in supplication cannot turn back the clock. Every thought, word and deed must be fully considered if one wishes to live an honourable life and especially so if one wishes to walk the path back Home. Each is accountable for their individual furrow in the field, responsibility cannot be passed on to another and the shelter of ignorance shall not be given, as one attempts to travel the steps of the mystic or wise-one.

Our individuality is a tool for the soul, it becomes the means for our life's journey and seeking of the unknown. As wise-ones, we grow to view our surroundings and interaction therein in such a way that we use the experience of perceived failures and successes accumulated to actively re-forge and temper the tool of Ego until it is comparable to that of the honourable hero of old.

This outlook may be seen in the following quotation:

"In Fate and the overcoming of Fate is the true Graal, for from this, inspiration comes and death is defeated." [149]

Where one then becomes the provider, warrior and priest of their own Wyrð.

---

148. John Donne, 1572-1631.   149. Robert Cochrane

The Knight at the Crossroads[150]

Will yours be a story told of spite, vitriol and misery?

Or one of immeasurable respect and honour throughout a life well-lived?

Or will yours be a tale not recounted at all?

Your story is being written as each moment passes, your words and deeds chosen each day forges that memory in which you shall leave behind.

150. Viktor Mikhailovich Vasnetsov. 1882. 'The Knight at the Crossroads', Public Domain, Wiki Commons License.

With 'memento mori' in mind and Wisdom ever-present in your heart, hold-fast to the knowledge that your Wyrð enables you in faith and sincerity to greet the new day with the notion that:

'Today is a good day to die'.[151]

151. Initially published online under the pseudonym 'Cunning Apostle' in 2012. (Wordpress)

PROVIDENCE

What is Providence? It is all things and no – thing. It has philosophical virtues and physical benefits too. Compiling a short list helps clarify this.

- Intervention by a higher being with regard to the future.
- Foresight and benevolent care.
- Of God, to the order of God.
- To foresee, to have forethought.
- Help and connection for advancement.
- Into the divine realms.
- Everything is a gift from the Gods, hence Providence.
- No event is random.

A providential 'god' then is one who 'sees' ahead, who anticipates (plans), and provides the necessary resources, offering us both protection and support. Thus all is in the hands of the gods; but not in a fatalistic sense. As humans, we prefer to believe we have Free Will, where the gods merely provide us with a deck of cards (this being our life), which is of course 'loaded.' Strategically 'fixed' so that each of us may successfully realise our destinies if we ride the tides of Fate 'provided' for us in 'life.'

> *"Bright Iðunna, Maid immortal!*
> *Standing at Valhalla's portal,*
> *In her casket has rich store*
> *Of rare apples, gilded o'er;*
> *Those rare apples, not of Earth,*
> *Ageing Æsir give fresh birth."*[152]

The Right Judgments must be meted to benefit fully from 'Free Will' – a sublime gift of the Gods to our erring humanity. If we fail them, we fail ourselves. Offering our Free Will in reciprocity, may seem a contrary option, and it could be logically argued why we should not return that gift to divine guidance. But which option truly presents the greater risk of failure.

How many are willing to surrender their trust – for that, for what they cannot see and do not know? Harder still is grasping our individual roles in the gods' great plans. Can any of say we comprehend all? I am happy to abnegate my eyes for theirs…. they alone see the 'Big Picture.'

We have to 'know' with absolute conviction how and why their governing of all manifest causes within their Master Plan provides our spiritual evolution. Material benefits are bountiful, but entirely incidental, (need rather than want or desire). And we must work for our own salvation. Orlog, the Fates and the gods merely set the stage; the rest is up to us.

152. 'VALHALLA' J. C. Jones

A Destiny of Life Eternal within the Supreme Matrix is the aim of all Initiates of The Higher Mysteries, and it must be understood as a blessing of the Highest Love, of a Father/Mother for their children.

Iðunna offers Loki Immortality[153]

153. *'Iduna Giving Loki the Apple.'*,1901 Signed "H. L. M." Source: Foster, Mary H. 1901. Asgard Stories: *Tales from Norse Mythology*. Silver, Burdett and Company. Page 69. Public Domain, Wiki Commons License.

It does involve risk:

• To Laugh, is to risk appearing the Fool.
• To Weep, is to risk appearing Sentimental.
• To Live, is to risk Dying.
• To Love, is to risk not being loved in return.
• To Hope is to risk Despair.
• To Strive, is to risk Failure.

Being a part of the Gods' plan is indeed a gamble. Once in play, everything is offered, what you need, when you need it, as if by coincidence. Everything is there already in place, in advance. Providence then, for the Gods, is the ability of know and plan for the future – our future. The tapestry is woven even before the thread is spun.

Wheel of Providence[154]

154. Unknown author/artist. *Virgin at the spinning wheel.* 1420-1430. Public Domain Reuse of PD-Art photographs.

Remembering though that knowing the future means knowing the past, knowing how to evaluate what has been, to become, and what is and what will be. Providence allows us to become who we really are, carefully unfurling the battle-field of the realised soul from the chrysalis of human form, from material ego, in order that each and everyone may know the 'self' and their gods.

What does this mean to the Individual?

When first undertaking research into this subject of Fate, it seemed to indicate 'coincidence' – our destiny. Also spare literature offers only a Christian context.

This leads to an assumption that Providence must therefore be only a Christian Mystery. But once this is overlooked, and a deeper view is sought, more may be gleaned and readily understood, bringing a profound realisation, this succour lies at the Hearth of all Gods. Often, chance meetings with someone that later fall away, may serve to bring us in contact with others with whom we share our entire lives in the greatest and most significant harmony and Companie.

We may sense the need sometimes that greater forces are at play and though we may not know what lies ahead, we can feel the pull towards the uncertain, and away from where we stand to continue an unfavourable 'Fate.'

Looking back, hindsight makes everything so clear and so obvious as to lead us to believe it could not have happened any other way. Had we ignored those insights, we stand to lose the greatest treasures. No matter how

Providence[155]

155. *O La Providence du Roi* by Jan van den Hoecke: Image credit –Jean-Pol Grand-mont – Public Domain, Wiki Commons License.

fleeting some relationships are, and no matter whether we drift away, we find in them, the deepest wonders to cherish.

Providence is a mystery not to be understood but to be aware of, to acknowledge, to learn from and adhere to. In life we all have things in life to do, and choices to makes. This may be called, chance, destiny or co-incidence – but for those who realise the guidance of a higher force in this, it is called Providence. And indeed, in the ancient world, Providence was deemed a Higher God. It is a symbiosis of trust and alignment. It is a surrender that requires consideration and awareness, a deep alliance at the soul level of being.

A Life Well-Lived

"To he who holds the Truth in his hand, more shall be handed; he who doesn't hold the Truth, even the little he has shall be taken away. Be your Self, especially when approaching death." [156]

How chaotic it all may seem, though once one raises awareness outside of their immediate environment, the dance of existence can be seen with greater clarity. To be a Watcher perched at the clearest vantage point, perspective is key in this round of Life. All too easily may we be caught in the bramble and thicket, all too easy it is to give in and accept the role of the victim held at the mercy of Man or the Divine. Too readily people offer themselves as the scapegoat, as if martyrdom in existence absolves them from any continuance of toil and strife.

Embrace all that Fate gives you!

'Take all that you are given..' ...after all She has offered us Life, the playground of Body, Soul and Spirit if one would forgive such an analogy. We have all been given a measure, an incomparable gift from the Sisters, and one that is enlivened and enlightened by Himself.

---

156. Gospel of Thomas

A gift demands a gift, one must not forget this, the time-honoured tradition of 'gyfu', whilst the gift of Life isn't a commodity which Man can give in reciprocity, as that is the prerogative of the Divine, what Man can give in return is a life well-lived.

'Give all of yourself'.

Within the peak of the Summer-tide, a vast array of colours and forms have seduced the senses up to this point. It can seem quite 'natural' to lose oneself to the glamour of form, to be intoxicated by the lushness of phenomenal existence, to be caught staring at the proverbial finger rather than the moon.

Such a vast array of form of existence is gifted so that Man is able to perceive every possible facet of the Divine. Are we looking at merely a form in itself or merely even a shadow cast by a fire's light on a cave wall?

Either view at the expense of the other is quite limiting, as our world of existence is indeed the prism in which the light of the Divine is refracted in order that it may be apprehended and known fully.

Truly, as when a landscape is explored in its entirety it may be better understood and respected a great deal more, so the smith tempers the Master's blade, knowing fully its constituent materials.

The maxim states that which is above is like that which is below, let us think also that that which is within is like that which is without.

Following this thread, as the outer form is experienced in a multitude of ways, are we to expect any lack in that which we experience internally? It is commonly considered that beauty is in the eye of the beholder, that not all which has place in the forge of existence appeals to the entirety of Man and their collective senses.

This view may be continued with the variation of experience as we follow the thread woven and measured for each of us. Not every experience, thought or feeling will always be considered as having merit, not every experience will seem pleasurable to those subject to it, just as not everything is pleasing to one's eye.

All serves a purpose; all experiences are gifted within our Wyrð. We are instructed to 'Know Thyself', yet how much of our Selves can we truly know if all that is experienced is pleasurable and stays within bounds of comfort? This would prove to give a very limited scope of life, and would show a very limited selection of our capabilities, our thresholds, our values and our aspirations.

With courage and fortitude shall life and all of the experiences it offers be faced, like the Hero on the quest shall adversary be welcomed, as trials will serve to aid the complete discovery of Self in every facet, just as the Divine is refracted through existence entire.

Shall one shrink away at every case of adversity?

No, let the words of ancestry stir forth the resolve to overcome:

'The lame can ride horses, the hand-less drive herds; the deaf can fight and do well; better blind than be burned; no one has use for a corpse.'[157]

The Heroic Quest[158]

157 Hávamál, 71.   158. *Gawain and the Green Knight,* Late 14th century. Unknown author/artist. Public Domain. PD Art.

Let us not be intoxicated by all that would distract us from the Great Work, whether it be the allure of material gain, self-pity or self-depreciation for that matter, let not our existence revolve around temporal dramas uncomfortable to the egoic self.

'I stood bravely in the middle of the world; I came in a body. I found them drunk! None were thirsty.'[159]

Instead let us thirst for all that life can throw at us, in order that we can better know ourselves and so, the Divine.

Let us lead a life well-lived.[160]

159. Gospel of Thomas.   160. Ulric 'Gestumblindi' Goding. Initially published online under the pseudonym "Cunning Apostle" in 2012.

ONE

"O Mother of the Universe,
This child is terrified by your naked Truth,
Your unthinkable blackness,
Your sheer infinity.
Please cover your Reality with a gentle veil"[161]

The One-Harrier first has to find one's self before He can seek the All. He is contradiction without contradiction, He is within humanity yet separate from it. Separated yet whole, He is the sword without a sword. He is humble, the aggression-less 'real' human being. Yet his weapons are his virtues. His strengths like his weaknesses are mercy and compassion, devoid of hatred, or malice, for his purpose is clear. His razor wit lends steels to all truths spoken, in irony and in despair. His enemies may sneer and bark, but always it seems, they are reliant upon the safety of being out of range.

Lapwings all.

They seek the Golden Halls from afar, their time is not this time. For this time is your time. There is no crooked

---

161. Ramprasad Sen

path, only crooked people. The road to the Mead Hall is as straight as a die, swift as an arrow, the road is treacherous only for the one not certain of his place there.

Lancelot at the Chapel[162]

The call is not heard by the ear alone. Hard to understand this journey. Subject to greater grief, we are wracked upon Her great wheel.

Yet we give ourselves up to Her cause, without hesitation. And so He will encounter wonders, coincidences that are to frequent to be so, He will find his true self for good or for bad, who will be the victor? The guide of the One Harrier is a reflection of the inner self. Only by truly understanding this blessed gift, that same gift She bestowed upon each of us as ever first breath was drawn, will any see the divine in all things, the radiance of Her bright face, there to guide truly.

It is the birth gift of a divine intercessor within the Source of All. It is always our solace on the dark road, the beacon in the shadow and the warm glow of the Hearth in the harshest of icy winds. The power it holds is beyond comprehension. But She will never deceive you, though She will always avenge Her own. As each footstep brings the pilgrim ever closer o'er the bridge, there to traverse and breach the Hel-Gates, the 'Naah' gates to Her Moated Castle beyond. Approached in gravid contemplation and sharpness of Mind…

Seek Her ardently with full and open Heart.
Know the keys. Take them. Use them.
Truth and honour are the weapons of choice.
There are many Halls and much to see.
Take all you are given, and become. ONE.
Death before dishonour.

Love eternal;
Beauty without flaw;
Truth without distinction.
Thrice Be Blessed
fff. Thoet Se!

Her Distant Castle[163]

163. *Burg Eltz,*' woodcut for a magazine article, *Once a Week*, volume 9, page 475.
17 October 1863, Internet Archive [Author] Thomas Sulman (1834–1900) Engraved by Joseph Swain and workshop (1820–1909) Attribution: Thomas Sulman, Public domain, via Wikimedia Commons license

ELEGY FOR THE FALLEN

What is to become of the Sown men of the Serpent's teeth,

Those that are, and those who yet aspire to be.

For all are one in the River of Tears.

All aspire to hold the light,

To become righteous before their Drighton Lord.

All seek that promised Grace and taste fair
Redemption's promise.

All desire to ascend the Tree and grasp the Emerald Stone,

To feel the flow of Virtue, coursing through blood and bone,

These mysteries as Pilgrims do all born of woman fair,
seek to know.

To reach into Her Void, to She, the Mother of All lives
and dies.

This is the Task. This is the Quest.

Hold fast to the 'Way.'

Guided by the alchemy of the Heart,

Be prepared to die.

Deny the Lie, follow only Truth.

Ken the Serpent – Sharpen your vision.

For his wizened teeth are sparse, and as each falls, Who then may summon fit warriors to stand for them.

Bitter is this loss; but grieve not.

Cherish fully the gift of life.

That Treasure will one day be reclaimed by the Old Dragon Lord.

'Til that triumphant rejoicing cometh –

Live each day as though it were your last - and prepare each day as:

A 'good day to die.'

Valkyrie[164]

164. *Brynhildr* by Robert Engels 1919. Public domain, via Wikimedia Commons license

Witchfather, A Life of Gerald Gardner.
Vol.1. Into the Witch Cult

Vol.2 – From Witch Cult to Wicca
by Philip Heselton

From the author of the highly acclaimed *Wiccan Roots*, this is the first full-length biography of Gerald Brosseau Gardner (1884-1964) – a very personal tale of the man who single-handedly brought about the revival of witchcraft in England in the mid 20th Century.

From his birth into an old family of wealthy Liverpool merchants, through an unconventional upbringing by his flamboyant governess in the resorts of the Mediterranean and Madeira, it tells how, having taught himself to read, his life was changed by finding a book on spiritualism.

During a working life as a tea and rubber planter in Ceylon, Borneo and Malaya, he came to know the native people and was invited to their secret rituals.

But it was only on his retirement to England, settling on the edge of the New Forest in Hampshire, that destiny took him firmly by the hand. Through various twists and turns involving naturist clubs and a strange esoteric theatre, he became friends with a group of people who eventually revealed their true identity – they were members of a surviving witch coven.

One evening in 1939, as the hounds of war were being unleashed, he was initiated into the 'witch cult' by these people, who called themselves 'the Wica'. Gardner was overwhelmed by the experience and was determined that the 'witch cult' should survive.

This book chronicles his efforts over the remaining quarter century of his life to ensure not only that it survived but that it would become the significant player on the world religious stage that it now is – '*the only religion that England has ever given the world*', in the words of Ronald Hutton, Professor of History at the University of Bristol, who calls it '...*a very fine book: humane, intelligent, compassionate, shrewd, and based upon a colossal amount of primary research*'.

Vol.1 ISBN 978-1-870450-80-5
Vol.2. ISBN 978-1-870450-79-9

Inventing Witchcraft
A Cast Study in the Creation of a New Religion
by Aidan A. Kelly

THE BOOK THEY TRIED TO BAN

When the first edition of this book was released, conservative Gardnerian Witches attempted to suppress it, claiming that it discredited their religion. Even though its first printing quickly sold out, the original publisher, faced with death threats and boycotts, agreed to abandon the project, and no other publisher has dared to reprint it before now.

NOW READ THE TRUTH

Dr. Aidan A. Kelly has thoroughly investigated the history, rituals, and documents behind the evolution of modern Witchcraft, and has concluded that Gerald Gardner invented Wicca as a new religion. Although Wicca claims to be a persecuted pagan religion dating from before the rise of Christianity, it draws upon controversial historical sources, modern occult practices, including those of Alistair Crowley and the Hermetic order of the Golden Dawn, 19th century translations of medieval grimoires, and the poetry of Gardner's priestess, Doreen Valiente.

EXPANDED EVIDENCE

This extensively revised edition contains new research, which was unavailable at the time, as well as detailed textual comparisons of Gerald Gardner's own manuscripts, magical books, and rituals that could not be including in the earlier edition. It includes contributions from people who helped Gardner create modern Witchcraft and looks at the sources of his inspiration. Both liberal Wiccans and religious scholars hailed the earlier book as a classic in the new field of Pagan Studies. This revised edition is a must-have for anyone interested in Witchcraft and modern religious history. Aidan A. Kelly received his Ph.D in theology from the Graduate Theological Union in 1980, in a joint programme in advanced humanities with the University of California, Berkeley. He has taught at the University of San Franciso and other colleges, and served for five years on the steering committee of the prestigious Group on New Religious Movements of the American Academy of Religion. He is well-known in academic circles for his argument that all religions begin as new religions. He is also a founder of the New Reformed Orthodox Order of the Golden Dawn, an eclectic Wiccan tradition, and of the Covenant of the Goddess, a national church for American Witches.

ISBN 978-1-870450-58-4

www.ingramcontent.com/pod-product-compliance
Lightning Source LLC
Chambersburg PA
CBHW051209090426
42740CB00021B/3427